AMERICAN JEWS & THE SEPARATIONIST —FAITH—

American Jews and the Separationist Faith is a joint
project of the Institute on Religion and Public Life
and the Ethics and Public Policy Center.

DAVID G. DALIN, an ordained rabbi, is associate professor of
American Jewish history at the University of Hartford, and a
member of the Editorial Advisory Board of the journal *First
Things*. He is the editor of *From Marxism to Judaism: The Collected
Essays of Will Herberg* and has contributed articles and reviews to
a number of publications, including *Commentary*, *First Things*,
This World, *American Jewish History*, *Conservative Judaism*, *Journal
of Reform Judaism*, *Religious Studies Review*, *Modern Judaism*, and
the *American Jewish Year Book*.

IRVING KRISTOL is publisher of *The National Interest* and co-
editor of *The Public Interest*.

The publication of this book has been made possible in part by
a grant from the JOSEPH MEYERHOFF FUND, INC.

AMERICAN
JEWS & THE
SEPARATIONIST
—FAITH—

The New Debate on Religion in Public Life

EDITED BY
David G. Dalin

AFTERWORD BY
Irving Kristol

ETHICS AND PUBLIC POLICY CENTER

The **ETHICS AND PUBLIC POLICY CENTER,** established in 1976, conducts a program of research, writing, publications, and conferences to encourage debate on domestic and foreign policy issues among religious, educational, academic, business, political, and other leaders. A nonpartisan effort, the Center is supported by contributions (which are tax deductible) from foundations, corporations, and individuals. The authors alone are responsible for the views expressed in Center publications.

Library of Congress Cataloging-in-Publication Data

American Jews and the separationist faith : the new debate on religion in public life / edited by David G. Dalin ; afterword by Irving Kristol.
p.   cm.
Includes index.
1. Judaism and state.   2. Judaism—United States.   3. Jews—United States—Politics and government.   4. Church and state—United States.   5. Jewish day schools—United States—Finance.   6. United States—Ethnic relations.   I. Dalin, David G.
BM538.S7A46   1992
296.3'877—dc20   92–27262 CIP

ISBN 0–89633–176–8 (cloth : alk. paper)

Distributed by:
National Book Network
4720 Boston Way
Lanham, MD 20706

3 Henrietta Street
London WC2E 8LU England

All Ethics and Public Policy Center books are produced on acid-free paper. The paper used in this publication meets the minimum requirements of American National Standard for Information Sciences—Permanence of Paper for Printed Library Materials, ANSI Z39.48–1984.   ♾ ™

Ethics and Public Policy Center
1015 Fifteenth Street N.W.
Washington, D.C. 20005
(202) 682–1200

For my brother and sister-in-law,
Rabbi Ralph Dalin and Hedy Dalin,
and my niece Aviva

Contents

Acknowledgments

T HE publication of this volume affords me a welcome opportunity to acknowledge my thanks to a number of people. A special debt of gratitude is reserved for Richard John Neuhaus, president of the Institute on Religion and Public Life and editor-in-chief of *First Things*, who invited me to help organize the "Judaism and American Public Life" symposium that appeared in the March 1991 issue of that journal, and who subsequently suggested that I expand that symposium into the present volume. I remain grateful for his continuing advice, encouragement, and friendship over the past several years, and for his role in transforming the idea for this book into a reality. I am also grateful to three other friends, Jonathan D. Sarna of Brandeis University, David Novak of the University of Virginia, and Midge Decter of the Institute on Religion and Public Life, who provided much advice and encouragement in the planning and editing of this volume, to which they are also contributors. Midge Decter also read and commented on my introduction; for her numerous constructive suggestions, I am additionally in her debt.

I remain indebted, as well, to several other friends on the staff of *First Things*, the Institute on Religion and Public Life, and the Ethics and Public Policy Center. James Nuechterlein, Matthew Berke, Davida Goldman, and Elizabeth Posey contributed much time and energy to the publication of both the original symposium and this expansion of it. George Weigel, president of the Ethics and Public Policy Center, graciously invited me to have this book included among the distinguished publications of the Center, and made several invaluable suggestions about its content. Carol Griffith, senior editor at the Center, carefully (and superbly!) edited the entire manuscript for publication.

A final note of thanks is due to Irving Kristol for his thoughtful "Afterword" and to *Commentary* for permission to reprint it.

I am dedicating this book, with love and gratitude, to my brother and sister-in-law, Ralph and Hedy Dalin, and my niece Aviva.

Introduction

DAVID G. DALIN

SINCE the 1940s, *at least*, most American Jews have conceived of religion and public life as being rigidly separate realms. They have steadfastly opposed the presence of any religious symbols and practices in the public arena. According to the prevailing liberal Jewish separationist faith of the 1950s and 1960s, Jewish survival and freedom are most secure where the wall separating religion and state is strongest and least secure where government and religion are intertwined.

For several decades, Leo Pfeffer, one of America's foremost scholars of church-state relations, has been the preeminent Jewish spokesman for this separationist faith. Pfeffer is staff attorney, and was for many years director, of the American Jewish Congress's Commission on Law and Social Action. He has argued more church-state cases before the United States Supreme Court than any other person in American history, and has done more than anyone else to shape and further the legal doctrine of church-state separationism.

The text at the heart of the debate is found in the first part of the First Amendment to the Constitution, which we habitually divide into two "clauses," the Establishment Clause and the Free Exercise Clause: "Congress shall make no law respecting an establishment of religion, or prohibiting the free exercise thereof." Whether that brief assertion is in fact one "religion clause," in which "no establishment" serves the goal of "free exercise," is very much at issue today.

Instead of embracing the "narrow" interpretation of the Establishment Clause, Pfeffer and those who share his views consistently invoke the "broad interpretation" espoused by the Supreme Court

1

in its famous *Everson* v. *Board of Education* decision of 1947,
wherein it claimed, quoting the words of Thomas Jefferson, that
the Establishment Clause "was intended to erect 'a wall of separation between church and state.' " Strict separationists believe that
the "intent" of the First Amendment is "to preclude any government aid to religious groups or dogmas." As Pfeffer argued in
Church, State, and Freedom, any government aid to religion, "even
on a nonpreferential basis," violates the Establishment Clause.

Beginning in 1948, with the landmark Supreme Court case
McCollum v. *Board of Education*, Pfeffer has led an unrelenting fight
against prayer and religious instruction in the public schools, state
aid to parochial schools, tax exemptions for churches and synagogues, and the presence of any religious symbol in public life. In
the 1948 case, the McCollums challenged the constitutionality of a
released-time program that used public-school classrooms for religious instruction during regular school hours. Pfeffer supported
their challenge in a "friend of the court" brief on behalf of the
Synagogue Council of America (an umbrella organization representing Orthodox, Conservative, and Reform rabbinic and congregational groups) and the National Jewish Community Relations
Advisory Council (NJCRAC, which represents a wide spectrum of
Jewish community-relations agencies, including the American Jewish Congress, the American Jewish Committee, and the Anti-
Defamation League of B'nai B'rith).

The decision of the Court in the *McCollum* case was that such
released-time programs were indeed unconstitutional. A month
after this decision, the Synagogue Council of America and
NJCRAC formed a Joint Committee on Religion and the Public
School (later the Joint Advisory Committee on Religion and State),
which, under Pfeffer's astute guidance, formulated public statements and drafted legal briefs in opposition to released and shared
time, government support for private religious schools, religious
observances in the public schools, and the teaching of religion
under the guise of "moral and spiritual values."

Like other immigrant Jews of his generation, Leo Pfeffer had
been taught by both Jewish history and his own experience to
embrace strict separationism as the only defense against what they
perceived to be a Christian-dominated state. For the separationists,

it became axiomatic that any religious influence in the public institutions of Christian America impinged upon the full citizenship of Jews. Only strict separation, they believed, could ensure the kind of free society and political climate wherein Jews, and Judaism, could flourish.

Pfeffer's view that "complete separation of church and state is best for the church and best for the state, and secures freedoms for both" seemed to most American Jews to be logically consistent and historically convincing. When the Supreme Court, in *Engel* v. *Vitale* (1962) and *Abington Township School District* v. *Schempp* (1963), outlawed state-composed prayers and state-sponsored Bible reading in the public schools, the overwhelming majority of American Jews applauded the decisions. Pfeffer proudly asserted in a 1966 address to the Joint Advisory Committee, "Our absolutist policy has now become the supreme law of the land through a series of decisions to which our test cases, briefs and other writing contributed substantially."

The Challenge of Will Herberg

But the separationist position did not go wholly unchallenged even in its heyday. In articles published during the 1950s and 1960s, Will Herberg and other Jewish thinkers began to call for a reassessment of the prevailing consensus that religion should play no role in American public life. The authors of the Constitution never intended to erect a "wall of separation," said Herberg. The Establishment Clause of the First Amendment had been profoundly misunderstood: although the Founding Fathers did not want to favor any single religion, they were not against helping all religions, or all religion, equally. "Neither in the minds of the Founding Fathers nor in the thinking of the American People through the nineteenth and twentieth century," wrote Herberg, "did the doctrine of the First Amendment ever imply an ironclad ban forbidding the government to take account of religion or to support its various activities."

Herberg was especially vocal in his criticism of liberal American Jews and their insistence that religion be rigidly distinct from public life. In several articles published during the 1950s and 1960s,

Herberg urged the liberal Jewish "establishment" to reassess this position. "The American Jew must have sufficient confidence in the capacity of democracy to preserve its pluralistic . . . character without any *absolute* wall of separation between religion and public life," he wrote in 1952. Eleven years later, frustrated by Jewish support for the 1963 Supreme Court decision banning Bible reading and recitation of the Lord's Prayer in the public schools, Herberg entered a plea for the restoration of religion to a place of honor in American public life. Writing in *National Review* he said:

> Within the meaning of our political tradition and political prac-
> tice, the promotion [of religion] has been, and continues to be,
> a part of the very legitimate "secular" purpose of the state.
> Whatever the "neutrality" of the state in matters of religion may
> be, it cannot be a neutrality between religion and no-religion,
> any more than . . . it could be a neutrality between morality and
> no-morality, . . . [both religion and morality being] as necessary
> to "good government" as "national prosperity."

"The traditional symbols of the divine presence in our public life," Herberg warned, "ought not to be tampered with."

During the 1960s, other prominent Jewish thinkers, such as professors Jakob J. Petuchowski of Hebrew Union College and Seymour Siegel of the Jewish Theological Seminary, and Milton Himmelfarb, editor of the *American Jewish Year Book*, began to eschew their earlier liberal faith in separationism, and to develop a strong Jewish conservative argument for the desirability of greater religious involvement in American public life. While supporting state aid to parochial schools and questioning Jewish opposition to public-school prayer, they (like Herberg) called for an abandonment of the Jewish separationist agenda in favor of a more pro-religion stance. Thus, writing in *Commentary* in 1966 on the subject of public aid to parochial schools, Himmelfarb argued:

> It is not true that freedom is most secure where church and state
> are separated. . . . Separationism is potentially tyrannical. . . . It
> is harsh to those who prefer nonpublic schools for conscience'
> sake; and it stands in the way of a more important good (and
> more important safeguard of Jewish security), the best possible
> education for all. . . . It is time that we [American Jews] actually

weighed the utility and cost of education against the utility and cost of separationism. All the evidence points to education, more than anything else, influencing adherence to democracy and equalitarianism. All the evidence points to Catholic parochial education having the same influence. . . . Something that nurtures a humane, liberal democracy is rather more important to Jews than twenty-four-carat separationism.

During the 1970s and 1980s, a Jewish neoconservative consensus began to emerge concerning the proper relationship between religion and politics, and the role of religious and moral values in shaping American public life. Himmelfarb, Siegel, Irving Kristol, and Murray Friedman, among others, all persuasively warned that an American moral and political culture uninformed by religious beliefs and institutions undermined the position of Jews and the health of a democratic society.

The Day-School Movement

One issue that forced a reexamination of the separationist hegemony for many was whether the government should give aid to parochial schools. During the 1960s and 1970s, Orthodox Jews had abandoned their opposition to such aid in the hope of obtaining funds for their own schools. They began to argue, as Catholics had before them, that education in a religious setting benefited not only members of their own faith but also the nation as a whole, and that money used to support secular studies at these schools should not be denied just because the schools also taught religious subjects. In 1965, when Congress debated the Elementary and Secondary Education Act, which proposed to extend $2.3 billion dollars in federal aid to the nation's elementary and secondary schools, Rabbi Moshe Sherer testified before Congress in support of financial aid to private and parochial schools. Sherer, the executive vice president of Agudath Israel of America, argued that Jewish day schools faced "extremely difficult financial circumstances," and that denial of tax aid to these schools would constitute "a discrimination which is not in accordance with basic American ideals." He vigorously urged the extension of federal aid to the 251 Orthodox elementary and secondary schools he represented.

Throughout the 1970s and 1980s, the growth of Jewish day schools outside the Orthodox community prompted some Conservative and Reform rabbis and educators also to rethink their earlier opposition to state aid. "The time has come," argued Seymour Siegel in *Sh'ma* in 1970, in an argument that he (and others) would reiterate many times over the following two decades, "for the Jewish community to revise its stand . . . and to support the public officials who are in favor of state aid to all schools, including parochial schools, day schools and yeshivoth":

> There is more and more realization in the Conservative movement that the strengthening of the Day School movement is essential for the maintenance of religious life. Even the Reform movement, once positively antagonistic, seems to be opening such schools, recognizing that they are vital to Jewish survival. So Jewish parents are now more sympathetic to the plight of Catholic parents. They have been claiming that without government aid for their parochial schools they were carrying a double load of taxation and that the special financial burden of supporting children in church-related institutions constitutes, in effect, a threat to their religious freedom.

In addition to abandoning their earlier opposition to state aid to parochial schools during the 1960s, Orthodox thinkers and communal leaders began increasingly, as Jonathan D. Sarna has noted, to cast doubt on the entire separationist approach to church and state, terming it "robot-like" and "unthinking." In the late 1960s, a group of young Orthodox Jewish lawyers and social scientists organized the National Jewish Commission on Law and Public Affairs (COLPA). Its purpose was to serve as a counterweight to the legal staffs of the American Jewish Congress and other separationist agencies in litigation concerning issues of religion and state. During the past twenty years, COLPA has appeared as *amicus curiae* in numerous church-state cases before the state and federal appellate courts, and the United States Supreme Court as well. Through COLPA's initiative, American courts have increasingly recognized that, although certain practices arising out of the requirements of Jewish religious law may conflict with society's normal practices, these requirements are entitled to reasonable accommodation.

COLPA has contributed to the development of a growing body of law, both judicial and statutory, relating to the accommodation of religious practices in America, as well as to a new and exciting debate on the relationship between religion and public life.

Religious Symbols in the Public Square

The issue of displaying religious symbols on public property has also been central to this new debate. Within the American Jewish community there has been a growing recognition that the triumph of strict separationism as a legal doctrine, with its promise to expunge any and all religious symbols from the public arena, may actually infringe upon the free exercise of religion cherished by American Jews. The 1986 U.S. Supreme Court decision in *Goldman* v. *Weinberger* is illustrative of this tendency. Simcha Goldman, an Orthodox Jew and ordained rabbi serving as a clinical psychologist in an Air Force hospital, normally wore a yarmulke at all times. He contended that an Air Force dress-code regulation that forbade the wearing of "headgear" indoors infringed upon his First Amendment right to free exercise of his religious belief. The Supreme Court, however, upheld the Air Force regulation: the First Amendment's free-exercise protection, ruled the Court, did not require the military to accommodate Captain Goldman's religious obligation. Implicit to the doctrine of church-state separation, which the Supreme Court enforced in this case, is the assumption that religious symbols, such as the yarmulke, while appropriate for private religious devotion in home or synagogue, have no legitimate place in any public institution, whether educational or military. The Supreme Court's denial of Simcha Goldman's free exercise of his religious obligation to wear a yarmulke is, it seems to me, a troubling example of what the Pfefferian ideal of strict separationism has wrought.

Another troubling example has been the unbending efforts of liberal Jewish organizations to keep religious symbols, such as the crèche and menorah, outside the public arena. Recently, however, as part of the changing debate generated by the Supreme Court case *Allegheny County, City of Pittsburgh, and Chabad* v. *ACLU*, the traditional opposition to the public display of religious symbols has been countered by a growing demand for "equal time" for the display of specifically Jewish religious symbols in the public square. This 1989 case challenged the constitutional propriety of placing a Hanukkah menorah in front of a public building or within a public park. Jewish opponents of these displays have argued that "since there is no religious need to place sacred symbols of any faith on public property . . . there is no religious need to be accommodated by government."

Other Jews, including the attorneys of COLPA, who made the argument before the Supreme Court for the public display of the menorah, believed that a compelling religious need does exist. Where religious symbols of differing faiths—e.g., the Hanukkah menorah and the Christmas tree—are displayed side by side, as in the *Allegheny* case, say these advocates, the government is not favoring one religion but rather is expressing equal respect for all religions. Promoting harmony amongst religious groups, they contend, is profoundly different from the "establishing" of one religion that the First Amendment seeks to protect us from. By giving a Jewish religious display "equal time" with a Christian one, Pittsburgh was showing the very neutrality with regard to all religions that the First Amendment was enacted to guarantee.

Exploring the New Debate

Should the once dominant and virtually unchallenged liberal Jewish alliance with strict separationists be abandoned, to be replaced by a new coalition with groups seeking to shape government law and policy in a pro-religion direction? Instead of fighting for the elimination of religious symbols and teachings within the public arena, ought Jewish leaders to be fighting for the "free exercise" of religion through laws and governmental programs that encourage rather than restrict the role of religion in public life? This is the new debate, and it involves the most substantial reexamination of Pfefferian separationism in many decades.

To explore this complex issue, the editors of *First Things* magazine and I asked a number of Jewish observers two questions: What ought to be the role of religion in American public life? How has your thinking on this question changed (if indeed it has changed)?

The resulting symposium on "Judaism and American Public Life," with sixteen participants, appeared in the March 1991 issue of *First Things*. Subsequently we decided to solicit the opinions of other American Jewish intellectuals and communal leaders on the same questions, and to publish the expanded symposium as a book. The thirty-eight contributors include rabbis, lawyers, academicians, Jewish community-relations specialists, and professional writers, who represent the entire political spectrum from liberal to conservative, and who identify with or represent the various religious denominations of American Judaism.

No longer can it be said, as it could in the 1940s and 1950s, that American Jewry speaks with one "official" voice on the issues of religion and public life. To be sure, a number of the contributors remain wedded to a strict separationist position on most, if not all, issues. But others seem uncomfortable with at least some aspects of that position. And several seem to share the new post-separationist faith of Rabbi Walter Wurzburger, first espoused ten years ago and reiterated in this volume, that in place of "excessive preoccupation with the Establishment Clause," greater attention should be given to the free-exercise claims of religiously observant Jews and other religious believers within American society. Instead of "clamoring for an impenetrable wall of separation," argues Wurzberger, "we should concentrate upon protecting the Free Exercise Clause, thus insuring that unpopular religious practices, such as accommodating Sabbath observers and serving kosher food in public institutions, will be safeguarded."

A growing minority of American Jews seem to have rejected the secular view that the interests of American Jews, and American Judaism, are best served by what Richard John Neuhaus called "the naked public square," one that is morally neutral. They think that religion has a legitimate place in American public life, that the Constitution does not embody what Justice Arthur Goldberg once described as "a brooding and pervasive devotion to the secular and a passive, or even active, hostility to the religious." Such views, though they cannot be said to represent a mainstream Jewish consensus, command greater intellectual force and weight than ever before.

1

Hadley Arkes

MANY years ago I heard a radio interview with a Unitarian minister who was trying to explain the tenets of his church. "Let me put it this way," he said to the interviewer. "The only time the words 'Jesus Christ' are heard in our church is when the janitor falls down the stairs."

American Jews have hardly been more sluggish in traveling the path of modernity and emancipating themselves from the texts and fables that were fashioned for more primitive minds in those days before religion became theology. Most of the people in America who count themselves Jewish are content these days to live lives that are not, shall we say, overburdened with theology. They come together to mark the Jewish calendar, they preserve the memory of the Holocaust and the worst trials of our people, and they are prepared to be summoned at any moment to the defense of Israel. Their life as a Jewish community is consecrated to the preservation of a Jewish people.

But the meaning of a Jewish people is increasingly detached from any notion of a people that finds its character in a covenant with God or a dedication to his laws. In fact, any serious discussion about God or matters theological is often regarded as rather indecorous and unsettling. In my own community, in a congregation filled with academics, it has ever been easier to bring people

Hadley Arkes is the Edward Ney Professor of Jurisprudence and American Institutions at Amherst College. He is the author of *First Things* (Princeton, 1986) and *Beyond the Constitution* (Princeton, 1990).

together to work on a Jewish cookbook than to consider the doctrinal points that define the Jewishness of the congregation.

A dozen years ago, in a national meeting of the American Jewish Committee, I made the case for restraining a band of Nazis from marching through a Jewish community in Skokie, Illinois. The response I received that morning was buoyant and confirming, and yet the American Jewish Committee finally backed away from the project of restraining the Nazis. The reasons were evident in the meeting and in the responses of Jews throughout the country. There were, in Skokie, many survivors of the Holocaust, but the passion for protecting those survivors was overborne by a deeper uneasiness over the prospect of restricting political speech. The concern to protect "our own" was modified or translated into the sense of a Jewish stake in the First Amendment. But this fastidiousness has not prevented American Jews from going to the rescue of other groups, to protect *them* from the symbols of assault. The same large-souled people who would not restrain the brandishing of swastikas apparently have no trouble with sustaining prosecutions for the burning of crosses—or even with using injunctions and restraining thugs in advance from the burning of crosses.

In the transfiguration of Judaism in America, it is the First Amendment and the Constitution that have become "our own." And we seem to have made them our own more than any other group; for more than any other group, we seem more earnestly concerned about injuries to the Constitution than injuries to our own people. Other groups may not experience the same conflict because they do not read the Constitution in the same way—in the way, for example, that makes no moral discrimination among the kinds of speech or the kinds of political factions that the Constitution was meant to protect. From the public face of American Judaism, we would infer that for many American Jews, the Constitution has become incorporated into the character of Judaism as a source of principles that may even override the texts of the Pentateuch.

But not, of course, the Constitution in its original texts—not the Constitution that offered protections for slavery and no votes for women—and not even the understanding of natural rights and "self-evident" moral truths that underlay the Constitution. What has become authoritative is the Constitution in its most modern, *liberal* rendering, and the most liberal rendering of all is the rendition that accords with the agenda of political liberalism.

After all, what is one to make of the passages that fill that embarrassing book of Deuteronomy:

> Then Sihon came out against us, he and all his people, unto battle at Jahaz. And the Lord our God delivered him up before us; and we smote him, and his sons, and all his people. And we took all his cities at that time, and utterly destroyed every city, the men, and the women, and the little ones; we left none remaining [Deut. 2:32–34].

Passages of this kind we decorously put aside as no longer consistent with what are called "Jewish values." And from what are those "values" drawn, those values that reject the notion of visiting punishment and death upon people without making discriminations between the innocent and the guilty? Apparently, they are drawn from a moral understanding, cultivated over centuries, and from a tradition of reflection that has been affected by Christianity and the Enlightenment.

The Constitution is preeminently the product of that tradition; but the liberal rendering of the Constitution marks an "advance"— a further radical step that has a more recent beginning. The training school of liberalism is now in the schools of law, and for liberal jurisprudence, the new age begins in 1965 with *Griswold* v. *Connecticut*, the decision on contraception and privacy that prepared the ground for *Roe* v. *Wade* and the "right to an abortion." Those decisions are now taken as the touchstone for liberal jurisprudence. As one professor was heard to remark, no theory of jurisprudence that gives the "wrong" result in *Roe* v. *Wade* could possibly be a valid theory of the law.

If the Constitution has become more authoritative than the Bible for many Jews and if the Constitution has become identified with the liberalism of the left, abortion has become the defining issue for the politics and jurisprudence of liberalism. That point became clear beyond cavil in the hearings over the nomination of Robert Bork to the Supreme Court. The Democrats had lost their constituency for redistribution and an expansion of the welfare state. The

Democrats had become the party of the courts; their mission now was simply to protect the courts as the judges imposed policies on abortion, busing, and the environment that could not gather support at the polls. What was at stake in the Bork hearings was the defense of *Roe* v. *Wade*—and how else to explain why the American Jewish Committee should even consider taking a position on this nomination to the Court? What distinctly Jewish interests were engaged in the appointment of Robert Bork?

The teachings of Jewish law have been set quite emphatically in opposition to abortion. On that point, the Orthodox have never suffered serious doubts. Granted, Jewish teaching has been far more equivocal, shaded with far more stray confusions, than the teachings of Catholicism on this matter. Hence the curious persistence of those assertions in the Talmud that the embryo during the first forty days is "mere liquid," and that the embryo does not form until forty days. But these passages may be dismissed more readily by grownups who understand that the science of embryology has moved well beyond the level of Aristotle's biology. Of more lingering mischief is the kind of teaching found, say, in Nachmanides: that a fetus attached to the mother is not yet a life with a standing of its own, with a claim to be protected by the law, because the child is not self-sufficient. That ancient mistake of moral reasoning seems to claim a more enduring credulity.

Still, as I say, the teaching of Jewish law has been set mainly, strongly, in opposition to the killing of unborn children, just as it has been set in opposition to euthanasia. But now, of course, the "privacy interest" in abortion has been made the ground for new claims of rights—to end the lives of aged, infirm patients and to withdraw medical care from newborn, retarded infants. In both of these instances, the same moral premises are engaged, and the same parties understand that the defense of *Roe* v. *Wade* is at stake.

And so each case rounds up the usual suspects: the same advocacy groups, the same facile lawyers from the ACLU, the same clusters of doctors and ministers. Each of these delegations finds a prominent Jewish presence in offering the brief and fueling the movement, and we can expect that these positions too will soon gather support among Jewish civic organizations. But the movement is sufficiently advanced already to make the point. The Jewish presence in our politics has now been associated with moral ends that find little tethering in the documents and the traditions distinct to Judaism, and the defense of Jewish interests is waged now in the name of policies that may be utterly at odds with the commands of Jewish law.

In my own congregation in Amherst (or the congregation that used to be mine), I discovered years ago one forbidden subject. I was often invited to speak to the congregation on questions of affirmative action or other matters of public interest. But it became clear that I could not speak about abortion without straining the community and dividing the congregation. The understanding seemed to settle upon me: the price of my membership in the congregation was to preserve my silence in the synagogue on the issue that I regarded, more surely with each passing year, as the gravest question of moral consequence before us. That unease would not be felt within every Jewish congregation. But it marks the tension that puts some of us in an adversary position right now to understandings that fix—unmistakably and unbendingly—the Jewish community in America.

A Catholic friend, dismayed that large numbers of Catholics were untutored in the teachings of their faith, was measuring the depth of ignorance. "Half of the Church is in heresy," he said, "and the other half do not know enough to know it." The melancholy commentary that may be offered now on the state of Jewish understanding in America is that if we could attain even this condition, we could count it as a notable advance.

2

JEROLD S. AUERBACH

FOR many years, precisely as long as Judaism was marginal to my life, the strict separation of religion and state made perfect sense. The separation principle provided ample camouflage, enabling Jews to stand together against the further Christianization of American public life, yet without asserting anything Jewish. Jews could privatize Judaism, and even trivialize it, while persuading themselves that they were staunch Americans defending the Bill of Rights.

Jews were trapped in a double bind. We claimed allegiance to an American "tradition" of religious tolerance, pluralism, freedom, and separation. But we certainly knew, long before each December 25, that in all but name the United States still was—as Supreme Court justice Joseph Story had once declared—"a Christian country." We worshiped at Jefferson's "wall of separation" without ever learning that the author of that famous phrase had drafted Virginia's "Bill for Punishing Disturbers of Religious Worship and Sabbath Breakers," or that the First Amendment was more a monument to federalism and to Protestant definitions of denominational autonomy than to religious freedom.

For Jews, strict separation became a convenient constitutional rationale for strict secularism. Who ever thought to inquire whether the very principle of separation might not be fundamentally Chris-

---

Jerold S. Auerbach is a professor of history at Wellesley College. He is the author of *Unequal Justice, Justice Without Law?*, and *Rabbis and Lawyers: The Journey from Torah to Constitution*.

15

tian? (It was Jesus, not Moses, who distinguished between what must be rendered to God and to Caesar.) In the Jewish historical tradition, religion and nationality were closely intertwined (as for many Israelis they still are). Nevertheless, we were Americans, and if that required a pledge of allegiance to a principle that undermined our own history and identity as Jews, we would gladly pay the price. Yet Jews were not fools, nor were we fooled. Separation promised protection, in education and politics, against further Christian encroachment. That was sufficient reason for our tenacious defense of it. In the naked public square, we could still pretend that the emperor—or perhaps the rabbi—was fully clothed.

None of this was clear to me at the time. Christmas was only a "national" holiday. Sunday was merely "a day of rest." Christians deserved to monopolize and control access to positions of public and private power. As Jews, accepting the Christian terms of emancipation, we would behave ourselves by tucking Judaism into our private closets. A double standard, surely, but so much a part of the natural American order that it could hardly be questioned.

Only after a year in Israel did I have a glimmer of comprehension that there was nothing neutral about any of this. In the Jewish state, I was astonished to discover, Jews were observant not only at home but also on the street—and rabbis were in the Knesset, as members, not chaplains. The Jewish calendar obliterated American holidays that were also Christian holidays. Menorahs and mezuzahs adorned public buildings. In Jerusalem especially, the silence of Shabbat and the solemnity of Yom Kippur were strengthened and deepened by the ample support of government authority. The separation of religion and state might make sense where a tiny Jewish minority needed the benevolence of an overwhelming Christian majority, but, wrenched from the American context, the terms of accommodation to Christian norms were starkly exposed.

Years later, sufficiently provoked by assorted life experiences to examine some cherished assumptions, I prepared a course on religion and the state and, for a book I was writing, read widely in American religious history. The Christian imagery that pervaded American history, from the Puritans to the present, was inescapable. Yet from constitutional centennial to bicentennial, successive generations of American Jews had been taught to believe that the fondness for "Old Testament" metaphors in American public discourse displayed the fundamental continuity between ancient Jewish and modern American values—when in fact these metaphors expressed a flourishing Christian triumphalism.

Similarly, the First Amendment, that constitutional beacon of religious tolerance, had merely deprived the new federal government of power in the realm of religion, while carefully reserving to the states ample freedom to preserve a Christian commonwealth within their borders, if they were so inclined. Ironically, the "original intent" of the Framers, the hallmark of recent conservative jurisprudence, still has no more passionate advocates than secular liberals who (like Justices Black and Douglas before them) look to Jefferson and Madison to support their own separationist preferences.

The role of religion in American public life is likely to remain what it has been: pervasively Christian, yet prudently concealed. In a country where 95 per cent of the population is nominally Christian, this continues to pose obvious problems for Jews—the more so now that the traditionally united front of Jewish support for strict separation has sharply fragmented. The enthusiastic advocacy of the Lubavitch Hassidim for menorahs on public property and public funds for yeshivas has shattered the once monolithic "Jewish" position on church-state issues. With their "establishment" battles securely won, Jews must now decide whether they can tolerate their own religious symbols in the public square, where there are already Christmas trees and crèches, or whether it remains too risky to demand the free exercise of Judaism, consistent with the promise of the First Amendment.

The more comfortable I became with Judaism, and with Jewish observance, the less I could defend the separationist position. Now, it seems a curiously American form of Jewish self-denial whose primary function is to separate religion from life, precisely contrary to Jewish teaching. I can no longer pretend that separation effectively neutralizes Christianity. The United States, after all, is a country whose history, calendar, language, and, more than occasionally, law reflect the Christian piety and purpose that framed so much of the American colonial and national experience.

Jews may find it uncomfortable to acknowledge this reality, for it undeniably separates them from the American mainstream. But if Jews do not intend to become even more assimilated than intermarriage, secular liberalism, and assorted other American temptations have already encouraged, their only alternative may be to assert vigorously their own distinctiveness as Jews. If the United States truly is as tolerant of diversity as it claims, then Jews should have nothing to fear from being themselves, in public and in private. If it is not true, then Jews should learn the limits and stop pretending otherwise.

In the end, the role of religion in public life is a prism through which to observe the survival—or atrophy—of American Jewry.

3

STEVEN BAYME

O VER a century ago Y. L. Gordon, the poet laureate of the Russian Jewish Enlightenment or Haskalah, advised his readers, "Be a man in the streets and a Jew at home." As Michael Stanislawski has recently argued, what Gordon was actually recommending was the modernization of Jewish culture—the integration of traditional Judaism with universal values of the Enlightenment. In practice, however, his advice was taken to mean strict separation between the private and the public sphere, the confinement of Judaism to the home and synagogue and its absence from the public square.

American Jewry has reversed this maxim. In the public domain American Jews are assertive. In defense of Israel or to protest the scheduling of school exams on Jewish holidays, American Jews feel few inhibitions about asserting their communal interests, even in the face of an unfriendly public. On elite campuses, observant male Jewish students—and lately some females ones as well—can be seen publicly displaying their *kippot*, or head-coverings, as a public demonstration of Jewish distinctiveness. Secular Jewish organizations, once the bastion of "keep your Jewishness private," increasingly employ traditional Jews intent on proclaiming Jewish values within the broader society.

The primary weaknesses of contemporary Jewish life are in the

Steven Bayme serves as national director of the Jewish Communal Affairs Department of the American Jewish Committee, and as director of its Institute on American Jewish–Israel Relations.

private domain. The same Jews who unabashedly defend Jewish communal interests in the centers of power in Washington find themselves incapable of articulating a language of Jewish content (let alone endogamy) to their children in the privacy of their homes.

Yet efforts to strengthen Jewish life today continue to focus on the public domain and, more specifically, on the place of Judaism in the public square. Opponents of "strict separationism" between church and state argue that the legal status quo in fact weakens Judaism by relegating it to private life. Others call for the public "marketing" of Judaism. Still others urge greater governmental assistance to Jewish institutions, particularly day schools.

These advocates assume that greater recognition of Judaism in the public square will lead to increased respect for Judaism as a faith, and will thereby enhance Jewish identity. Yet their well-intentioned proposals appear to ignore the real weaknesses of Jewish life. Whether Jews have the right to wear the *kippah* in the U.S. Air Force may be of concern to some, though the *kippah* has no standing in Jewish law. But to assume that such "rights" will foster Jewish tradition among those uncommitted to it is simply wrong. Similarly, advocates of public funding to Jewish institutions downplay or ignore the question whether such funding will mandate diminution of the distinctive content of Judaism taught within these institutions. Finally, the experience of Jewry in Britain, where an established church does exist, indicates that the presence of organized religion in the public square translates into marginal benefits for Jewish culture, e.g., reduced day-school tuitions, but often carries as its price a diminished capacity to assert publicly Jewish values and communal interests.

Allocating a greater role to religion in the public arena may very well enhance the degree of comfort for traditional Jews in American society. It may also raise issues of Jewish consciousness among those who know they are Jewish but have little idea what that means. However, it will have little effect upon the truly critical issues of continuity and quality in Jewish life. The major problems that Jews confront—increased intermarriage, declining Jewish cultural literacy, and sizable communal erosion and disaffiliation—stem not from the weakness of Judaism in the public arena but from the absence of Jewish content in the home and the consequent attenuation of private Jewish identity. Therefore, efforts to enhance Jewish life ought to be aimed at enabling Jews to partake of the joys of Judaism in their private lives, rather than at marginal—and possibly hurtful—initiatives to weaken church-state separation.

To be sure, there is a legitimate role for religion in the public square, but it is one that may be filled by public education rather than legislation. Jews would do well, for example, to advocate the presence of realistic and appropriate Jewish characterizations in the popular media so as to communicate positive images of Jewish private and public life. Until very recently, the only Jews portrayed on television were characters unable to assert any positive values— let alone joys—of leading a Jewish life.

Moreover, Jews possess a rich tradition that may profitably be applied to the great social and ethical issues of the day. All too often this has been done selectively, to validate a preconceived position. These practitioners of proof-texting are likely to elicit ridicule from knowledgeable scholars rather than enhanced respect for Judaism.

Orthodox Jews cite Jewish tradition in an authoritative and absolutist manner. Their message, too, invites societal rejection, for most Americans, and certainly most Jews, simply do not accept the binding authority of tradition.

Rather, what is necessary is honest and constructive engagement with Jewish sources, an encounter that will enable Jews to measure the salience of their tradition in modern times. The engagement itself would stimulate rethinking of what it means to be Jewish, for it would underscore not only the degree of consonance but also the conflicts between Jewish tradition and American values. Jews would be challenged to ponder the meaning of a distinctive Jewish identity and a distinctive American Jewish synthesis.

The overall impact on society would also be positive without furthering the attenuation of church-state boundaries. American society can well benefit from an overall climate in which religious norms are articulated in a persuasive and intelligent fashion. Jewish teaching can contribute to a climate in which Americans take the positive values of all religions more seriously.

An example is the abortion debate. Jewish organizations have, with few exceptions, advocated a pro-choice position and have cited

Jewish sources that at times permit and even mandate abortion. Virtually absent from the public pronouncements of Jewish organizations are statements of the moral gravity of abortion in Jewish tradition, its permissibility only in the most extreme of circumstances, the preferability of adoption, and the unequivocal rejection of abortion on demand, of abortion as an alternative form of birth control, and of the claim that "no one can tell me what to do with my body." An honest and open encounter with Jewish tradition could well result in a pro-choice position that communicates the rich array of Judaism's teachings on abortion. This could help to create a climate of opinion in America in which the legal availability of abortion underscores rather than detracts from the relevant moral questions.

A generation ago the sociologist and theologian Will Herberg wrote that Judaism had attained equal status with Protestantism and Catholicism in the panoply of American religions. However, Herberg cautioned that this status did not really mean very much, for all three faiths had become bland. The challenge to American Judaism today is not to overcome the barriers between church and state, barriers that have served Jews well. Rather, all religions should feel free to articulate their distinctive content, to ask what are their meaningful contributions to American life, and thereby to overcome the apparent blandness, and even more the moral relativism, that so many perceive in contemporary religious life.

4

MATTHEW BERKE

SEPARATION of church and state has been a good policy for Americans generally and for American Jews in particular. I include in that judgment at least some of the decisions by the U.S. Supreme Court in the past five decades, such as the banning of common prayer in public schools. That said, I must add that I have grown increasingly uneasy over the years with the absolutist position concerning religion and public life, i.e., the "strict separationism" held by many Americans, including a large number (probably a majority) of Jews. On this account, the public realm is supposed to be totally "neutral" with respect to religion; religious language is taboo in public discourse, as are religious symbols on public property; and public education and government policy are required to be impartial not only toward religions, but also toward religion and irreligion.

This sort of separationism, it seems to me, is involved in practical and theoretical contradictions that have made it intellectually untenable, or at least highly problematic. While it may think it seeks only neutrality toward religion, strict separationism in fact evidences a certain *hostility* toward religion—the effect of which is to deprive society of necessary moral and spiritual resources, to misinterpret the history of our culture, and to provoke anger and resentment among those who never consented to making our public life a "secular" enterprise.

I believe that Jews, like all other American citizens, suffer from

---

Matthew Berke is the managing editor of the journal *First Things*.

the unhappy consequences of a "naked public square." I recognize that Jews are understandably wary about the potential for discrimination by the Christian majority in a theologized public square. Now, however, it seems to me that in steering between the Scylla of atheism and the Charybdis of theocracy, we are moving too close to the rock of atheism and nihilism. That is now the greater threat to Jewish values and life in America.

I do not presume to have a set of policy prescriptions or legal briefs for bringing some ideal measure of religion into public life. Although I am loath to see a rush of religious "enthusiasm" and zealotry into the public square, I hope that rational, civil, and decorous expressions of the religious sensibility will be allowed greater compass in public affairs and discourse. The concerns expressed here are only tentative first thoughts, representing part of a potential agenda for Jewish leaders and organizations to consider, possibly in a dialogue with sympathetic Christian leaders and organizations.

Everyone seems to agree that there is a moral crisis among the nation's youth: an epidemic of crime, drugs, sexual immorality, and out-of-wedlock births. On a less urgent but still important level, it is recognized that there has been a general decline in manners, achievement, and ambition. In short, the moral crisis of today's youth is about corruption of character and loss of values. Comprehensive secularism has led not to "sweetness and light" but to a howling wilderness of the spirit and psyche. This crisis surely represents a threat to American society at large, and to Jews in particular, since, as a minority, we are likely to become victims when civilization gives way to barbarism.

There is a widespread sense (among Jews as well as non-Jews) that America's schools should "do something" to remedy the situation—usually, that schools should start teaching values again. Yet it seems to me that public schools are singularly ill equipped for this task. In the first place, ethical instruction in public schools must be administered from a purely "secular" standpoint—without reference to religious belief or authority. The theoretical problem with this, one that has been insufficiently appreciated, is that "secular" does not represent "neutral." Though many of the specific precepts of secular moral instruction may not contradict religious teaching, the overall idea of moral education abstracted from the complex of life, including its religious dimension, *does* contradict most religious traditions. To compel pupils to receive moral instruction from some artificial secular standpoint seems to me to be a violation of conscience prohibited by the Free Exercise Clause of the First Amendment.

Besides being unconstitutional and unfair, such instruction also runs into a practical difficulty: it tends to be vacuous and ineffective. It is true that morality can be taught without reference to religion insofar as ethical precepts can be stated without reference to their theological basis. However, the real process of character-formation involves not merely an absorption of precepts, but also the general orientation of the soul in which the ethical life is integrated with "the good life" in its broadest sense, so that morality becomes a matter of aspiration as well as exhortation. An ethical consciousness must be a vital part of life; this truth is neatly expressed in Matthew Arnold's summary of the ethical value of religion as "morality lighted by emotion." For the vital integration of morality, reason, and emotion to occur, it is necessary to appeal at the deepest level of conscience and aspiration, and to a person's ultimate sense of reality—areas that are off-limits to the state, including state schools.

If we are serious about values and moral instruction, there are some steps that might help. We could establish in public policy the use of vouchers or tax credits for parents sending their children to religiously affiliated schools where serious moral education can take place. Within the existing public-school framework, it might be helpful to expand the use of "released time," in which students may voluntarily receive religiously based moral instruction from clergy of their choice. How to accomplish this without being disruptive and divisive poses serious problems, and dealing with them is a task of enormous importance. For if, in fact, we want public schools to facilitate moral education, *true* separationism requires that the state defer to the religious institutions in matters of conscience and internal motivation. The hegemony of a generic account of ethics and conscience should be resisted as vigorously as the establishment of an explicitly theological account.

Insofar as government can legitimately facilitate moral education, it should *not* make direct money payments to churches and synagogues, nor should it grant anything like establishment status to any sect or family of faiths. However, it seems right and proper to me that public institutions, schools in particular, make a habit of acknowledging (rather than usurping) religion's role in character formation and moral instruction. Such acknowledgment is important, because lessons and ideas usually become ingrained when people find them confirmed by a variety of authoritative sources. This is why, for instance, it is so important for children to feel the authority of two parents rather than one whenever possible—plus teachers, clergy, community leaders, and the like. In view of this need for multiple confirmation, what can our youth think when religious perspectives alone are excluded from the otherwise raucous pluralism in their schools? And the public school is hardly the only institution that practices a stony silence and indifference (if not hostility) toward religion. The unique isolation of religion among American institutions seems to me a perversion of non-establishment and separationist doctrine.

Along similar lines, it might be wise for the social philosophy of American Jews to accommodate itself to more public use of religious symbols and language. I confess to a degree of trepidation here, but it does not seem to me that the presence of crèches and Christmas trees on public grounds, or the singing of Christmas carols in school programs, represents in all cases a threat to Jewish citizens or a diminution of their religion in relation to Christianity—especially in those communities and schools that are attentive to Jewish feelings and display Jewish symbols as well. The point is, we are a society that goes to great pains to recover its various "roots" and to celebrate the contributions of women and minorities and ethnic groups and professions. In all fairness, we must find a way to recognize and affirm the Christian tradition as part, indeed the major formative part, of the general inheritance that we call Western civilization.

Jews can come to a realization of this imperative either by self-regarding prudence or by intellectual honesty. By the logic of the former, we should not offend our Christian neighbors when we need to cultivate as much good will as possible for the common good of our own society and also for the sake of Israel. In any case, it seems imprudent for a tiny minority (2 to 3 per cent of the population at most) to have such a highly conspicuous cadre of strict separationists in powerful positions, playing the role of the Grinch at Christmas time by swooping down and eliminating holiday decorations.

That is a simple consideration of prudence. A more lofty one is that most of us, as Jews, hardly know ourselves or have a sense of Judaism that is not in some way tied up with our experience as cultured members of Western civilization, which is Christianized not only in an explicitly religious sense but also in the pathos and longing of its secular consciousness, as exemplified in its literature and art. Liberal democracy, humanism, even (ironically) the separation of church and state—all emerged from the matrix of a self-consciously Christian civilization. Jews have been able to respond enthusiastically to these cultural and political developments, in part at least, because they resonate with our own traditions and hopes. The Jewish embrace of, and contribution to, Western culture is testimony to a shared inheritance and spirit between Jews and Christians (even if there is not a Judeo-Christian tradition in the strict sense). If this Christian civilization has been involved in all manner of "crimes, follies, and misfortunes," including terrible atrocities against Jews, it has also nourished Jewish life; for evidence, compare the intellectual and religious development of European Jews with that of Jews in the Muslim lands of North Africa and Arabia.

I do not pretend to have answered every objection that might be raised to my suggestions. I do think, though, that we must begin to think about these questions free of a reflexive, often false, separationism. To a degree that would have been unimaginable in the past, it is now possible for Jews and Christians to engage in dialogue with real possibilities for mutual understanding. We must try harder to understand the perspectives and needs of the non-Jewish (principally Christian) majority. But before engaging in serious dialogue with others, we must first reevaluate our interests and ideas among ourselves.

5

J. DAVID BLEICH

J UST short of one hundred years ago, in *Church of the Holy Trinity v. U.S.*, a justice of the U.S. Supreme Court declared that "this is a Christian nation." Today students of constitutional law find that statement, if not embarrassing, at least quixotic. But at the time it was written, the learned author found no contradiction between that pronouncement and the (anti-)Establishment Clause of the First Amendment. At issue before the Court was an anti-immigration statute. The declaration was in support of a finding that "the common understanding of the terms labor and laborers does not include preaching and preachers." Lest anyone assume that clergymen actually work, the Court found it necessary to add that it would be unthinkable to assume that Congress in the anti-immigration statute intended to bar an invitation to an Anglican clergyman to minister to the religious needs of U.S. citizens.

But the declaration resonates with a more profound meaning. It clearly reflects a literal interpretation of the Establishment Clause as prohibiting only an established state church, and in no way precluding governmental preferment of religion and religious values. The authors of the Constitution certainly envisioned a Christian nation, *de facto* if not *de jure*. Indeed, the Bill of Rights did not at all interfere with the ongoing relationship with established religions that then existed in nine of the thirteen states. Quite to

J. David Bleich is the Herbert and Florence Tenzer Professor of Jewish Law and Ethics at Yeshiva University. He is the author of *Contemporary Halakhic Problems* (3 vols., Yeshiva University Press).

the contrary, the First Amendment was designed to prevent the establishment of a *national* church that would effectively supplant the churches established by the various states. As a matter of historical fact, the Bill of Rights was made binding upon the individual states, rather than upon the federal government exclusively, only after the various churches had long been disestablished.

To restate the age-old question: Has this been good for the Jews?

Historically, few have suffered more than Jews from the corrosive effects of government entanglement in matters of religion. Yet in a bygone age, more than a few rabbinic luminaries actively supported the Russian tsar over Napoleon, preferring the very real evils of religious oppression over the free-thinking ways of the Enlightenment. The underlying *angst* is pithily reflected in an ancient Yiddish maxim that I first heard as a child from my great-grandmother: "When you are riding in a horse and wagon and pass the door of a church, if the driver does not cross himself, get off immediately!" That admonition had nothing to do with theology and everything to do with safety and survival. The Jew understood that his own security demanded that the non-Jew profess a religion—and that for such purposes, any religion is better than none. Voltaire, a doctrinaire atheist himself, believed that atheism was safe only for intellectuals. He is reported to have said, "I want my lawyer, tailor, valets, even my wife to believe in G-d. I think that if they do I shall be robbed less and cheated less."

Our society tends to equate legality with morality. That which is legal is *ipso facto* moral; that which is illegal is immoral. The liberties and constraints enshrined in the Bill of Rights become, not simple constraints upon governmental authorities, but societal mandates. Who has not heard the argument that someone like the late Meir Kahane must be granted the pulpit because everyone is entitled to freedom of speech? Or that public funds must be made freely available for abortions because every woman enjoys a constitutionally protected right to personal autonomy? The elemental distinction between governmental interference in personal freedoms and societal promotion of moral values has, in the minds of many, become blurred beyond recognition.

One result of the constitutional separation of church and state is a certain embarrassment about the recognition of religion and religious values in public affairs. If a religious denomination has strong views on a particular public issue, it may be sure that its position will be dismissed as sectarian and hence unworthy of serious attention. Values nurtured by religious conviction are to be left at the church or synagogue door; they are not to influence or even inform public debate. To paraphrase a Jewish writer of the Enlightenment: "Be G-d-fearing in private, but an agnostic in public."

But separation of church and state does not require a hermetically sealed wall. Justice William Douglas, writing for the majority in *Zorach* v. *Clauson*, declared, "We are a religious people whose institutions presuppose the existence of a Supreme Being. . . . The First Amendment . . . does not say that in every and all respects there shall be a separation of Church and State. . . . We find no constitutional requirement which makes it necessary for government to be hostile to religion and throw its weight against efforts to widen the scope of religious influence."

Jewish interests are served not nearly so well by the Establishment Clause as by the Free Exercise Clause. In general, we have taken the Free Exercise guarantees for granted but have been vigilant in defending the Establishment Clause. The organizational representatives of the Jewish community have been remarkably successful in calling attention to the slightest compromise of the latter. Yet we were caught totally off guard by the 1990 Supreme Court decision in *Employment Division* v. *Smith* that effectively turned the Free Exercise Clause into an unarmed sentry.

A tension always existed between the two clauses. After all, the immunity from government intervention putatively guaranteed by the Free Exercise Clause is itself a form of "establishment," not of any particular religion but of all religions. Religion was favored in the sense that government dared not tamper with religious practices in any way, other than for reason of compelling state interest.

No more! *Smith* allows religion no quarter. No longer is religion constitutionally privileged. As long as religion is not singled out for restrictive treatment, government may ignore religious sensitivities completely in its regulation of the social weal. If any given jurisdiction wishes to forbid consumption of alcohol, it need make no exemption for even the smallest quantity of low-alcohol *kiddush* wine. No longer may a juror demand to be excused from jury duty on a holy day as a matter of right. No longer may a witness or a litigant refuse to remove his skullcap in a courtroom as a matter of right. No longer need zoning boards seek cogent reasons for banning houses of worship in residential areas. Any state can prohibit a *mohel* from performing circumcision by demanding that it be performed by a licensed physician. Any state can effectively bar kosher slaughter simply by demanding the stunning of all animals. The list could go on and on and on.

The Court probably did not fully appreciate the implication of its decision in *Smith*. It almost certainly did not appreciate the constitutional catastrophe it has created for Jews.

6

NAOMI W. COHEN

S EVERAL implications of this symposium leave me uneasy. For one, I don't see that the formation of the National Jewish Commission on Law and Public Affairs (COLPA) heralded a major break in mainline Jewish defense of strict separation. While COLPA labors for matters like state aid to parochial schools, the rights of Sabbath-observing Jews in the work force, and even the legality of the *eruv*, issues on which most Orthodox Jews agree, the Rabbinical Council and the Union of Orthodox Jewish Congregations remain under the separationist umbrella of the National Jewish Community Relations Advisory Council (NJCRAC) and the Synagogue Council of America (with registered qualifications in regard to parochaid and to litigation against menorahs on public property). Officially, therefore, the Union of Orthodox Congregations no less than its fellow agencies endorses NJCRAC's stand against public religious symbols, and it reaps the benefits of both the Orthodox and the secular defense network.

My second and more serious reservation concerns the implied assumption that Jewish behavior can arrest or undo the rampant evils of secularism. That in turn seems to attribute to Jews an inordinate responsibility for having unleashed those evils in the first place. To be sure, Jews as a group may be more secular than other Americans, and Jews have labored arduously through the courts for

Naomi W. Cohen is Adjunct Distinguished Service Professor of American Jewish history at the Jewish Theological Seminary. Her latest book, *Jews in Christian America* (Oxford University Press), deals with the Jewish stand on church-state separation.

a secular government; but the justices who decided the landmark cases of *McCollum* (1948), *Engel* (1962), and *Schempp* (1963) were Christian, as were the Congresses that rejected prayer amendments. In nineteenth-century America, religious zealots charged Jews, along with "infidels," "papists," and "atheists," with undermining the religious foundations of a Protestant nation. In the twentieth century the taunt of secularism, often equated with un-Americanism, has long resonated. At all times it has added grist to anti-Semitic mills.

Finally, I doubt very much that religious trappings in the public square—particularly if, to avoid giving offense, they are watered down to some bland nondenominational forms—can rid the nation of its monumental social problems. American history from the very beginning abounds with examples of plans and designs, none of which achieved marked success, to revamp the "godless" public school and to inculcate an awareness and appreciation of religious values. (It should be noted that Jews too debated the issues early on. Over a hundred years ago the *American Hebrew*, a Conservative weekly, wrote that secular schools were abhorrent, worse than "any form soever of religious fanaticism." Concluding that the teaching of morals divorced from religion was impossible, it suggested that some way be found to teach the doctrines common to the major religions, e.g., the existence of God, man's responsibility to his Creator, and the immortality of the soul.)

But even if the point on social improvement is conceded—and personally I would applaud any melioration generated by religion—the question of an appropriate Jewish posture remains. As I see it, the Jewish community has two broad options. One is to continue along the fixed lines of strict separationism. Nineteenth-century Jewish leaders committed themselves to the goal of maintaining a community of believers under a secular government. The alternatives to the privatization of religion appeared downright menacing. Religion, as Jews said, came with a label, and public religious forms were Protestant or at least Christian. In light of their bitter experience at the hands of Christian states, Jews sought their security in a non-religious (= non-Christian) state by fighting for secular schools and against laws and symbols that deferred to Christian beliefs or sentiments. To the extent that American courts and legislatures agreed, that posture, strict separationists claim, increased Jewish security and "at-homeness."

That approach, however, has glaring weaknesses. Attempts to keep religion out of politics were and are both unnatural and unsuccessful. Moreover, the coordinate goal of a community of believers largely fell by the wayside as Jews replaced religious spokesmen with secular ones and found surrogates for religion in philanthropy, liberal politics, or aid to Israel. It can be argued that separationism is not responsible for secularism, or that an advocate of a secular government is not necessarily a secularist (even Leo Pfeffer sent his children to Jewish day schools). But the energy, resources, and emotional frenzy of the separationist battle were never equaled by a commitment to the preservation of a vibrant Judaism. Passively if not actively, Jewish defenders abetted the secularization of their community. Finally, Jews should remember that no matter how secularized they become, or how separate the orbits of church and state, they will still be regarded as Jews. The number of "Christian secularists" notwithstanding, the Christian component of American culture will stand; the President will continue each year to light the Christmas tree but hardly the Hanukkah menorah.

The second option is to accept religion in the public square and to use religious beliefs as guides for social action. Here too there are conflicting factors. Thoughtful Jews need little reminder that programs of religion-in-general or of moral and spiritual values have been in the recent past, and most likely will be in the future, often interpreted as licenses for propagating Christianity. They also know that even in a free religious market, a menorah and Judah the Maccabee lack the attractiveness and appeal of a Christmas tree and nativity scene. On the other hand, it has been argued that second place is the best that a minority in exile can expect. To be sure, most Jews would reject out of hand the belief that America is *galut*, but the recognition of finite limits to the acceptability of Jews and Judaism does have its practical uses. It can help individual Jews to measure perceived insults by the Christian majority in broader perspective, and it tempers an obsessive communal fixation on separationism. Indeed, an admission of the need for public religion could force Jews, if only out of pride, to rank their spiritual needs and the reinvigoration of their faith as their first priorities. That alone would be a most welcome development.

I will not speculate on how well American Jews will continue to grapple with the question of public religion and its relation to specifically Jewish needs. I am not very sanguine about the results of either option I have advanced, but admittedly I start with a *galut* mentality.

7

BARRY D. CYTRON

D URING my first year in the rabbinate, I eagerly accepted an
invitation from an Iowa legislator to offer the opening prayer
at an upcoming House session.

On the appointed day, I drove to the state capitol on the other
side of Des Moines, where I was greeted warmly and ushered to
the dais. Looking over the thinly populated floor of fatigued but
graciously attentive legislators, I delivered a slightly altered version
of the "Prayer for Our Country" written by the well-known Tal-
mudist Louis Ginzberg for the Conservative movement's prayer-
book.

Later that week I bumped into a congregant at the grocery store.
"Well, Rabbi, how's it going?" he asked. "You finding your way
around town all right?"

I told him about giving the invocation at the House Chambers.

"H'mm. That must have been nice," he replied. "The next time
you get such an offer, I've got a terrific prayer you could use: 'O
God—separate church from state. Amen!' "

Nearly two decades later, I see that this unsolicited advice reflected the way many Jews feel about the place of religion in
American public life. That is especially true for those of us who
have lived in a region, such as the upper Midwest, with a sparse
Jewish population. Here in the Midwest, Jews typically constitute
less than 1 per cent of the citizenry. They have fought for decades

Barry D. Cytron is a rabbi at Adath Jeshurun Congregation in Minneap-
olis, Minnesota. He also serves on the faculty of Macalester College and
the University of St. Thomas.

to achieve civic parity in such settings. At one time, that struggle led them to champion the complete withdrawal of religion from the public domain, while simultaneously they were pleased with any form of "official recognition" for Judaism. Members of my community, for example, vigorously supported the drive of communal defense organizations to keep every religious practice out of the schools, yet were nonetheless proud when their rabbi delivered an invocation at a public gathering.

The sort of "recognition" that comes through such public displays of piety seems less necessary for Jewish self-respect today than in an earlier era. Now that there are many other means by which Jews in this country gain esteem, to insist that their rabbi get "equal time" no longer seems as important.

We are better off if we forgo any such public-relations gains, which are quite ephemeral, rather than allow ourselves to be enticed into some enterprise that might legitimate the intrusion of other religious *practices* into the public domain. The most persuasive reason for maintaining the "wall of separation" is that in places like Iowa and Minnesota, wherever Jews constitute the slimmest of minorities, being embraced by the state even on the most benign level will inevitably lead to being smothered by the state and its huge Christian majority. One Hanukkah menorah, no matter how large and prominently positioned, cannot possibly overcome that majority.

Yet it is more than just community struggles against such odds that have made so many wary of what can result when religion and the state cozy up to each other. For now we see what can happen to a modern state when that does occur, and it makes us more nervous than ever. That state, of course, is Israel, which is a potent teacher of what ensues when one religious point of view succeeds in getting a hammerlock on society.

To be sure, it is not altogether clear what it would mean for religion to be absent from Israeli public life. It is, after all, the PLO, and not the Jews, who seek to make that land "a secular state." Nonetheless, if ever there were a good case for a reliable barrier between religion and state, Israel is it. And if ever there were a motivation to heed the warning of a long-ago sage named Rabban Gamliel, the doings of Israel's political parties provide it. Two millennia ago, that eminently practical rabbi taught: "Be wary of the government, for they befriend you only for their convenience. They seem like allies when it benefits them, but they never stand by you when you are in need." It has taken some ultra-orthodox rabbis to prove how prescient that sage was. His words are still worth hearing, both in Israel and in America.

As for the view voiced by some that religion can be made more effective only when officially allowed into the public domain, I am reminded that several years back, "outreach to the unchurched" was touted as a means of rescuing the numerically declining American Jewish community. The argument then went that the only way to counter increasing assimilation and loss of Jewish commitment among those born Jewish was by slick new efforts to bring in new Jews from the massive numbers of those with no religious identity. While there are many good reasons to engage in "outreach," doing so because we are unable to hold our own is not one of them. That is like turning up the flow in the water faucet instead of stopping the leak.

Likewise, if we feel that what is happening inside our churches and synagogues is not effective enough, and that the church and synagogue are not as persuasive as they might be, the way to remedy those deficiencies is not by taking over the streets so that we have a larger territory in which to hawk our wares. Instead, we ought to figure out how to do a better job within the walls of our synagogues and churches, with the hope that our congregants will then take what they have learned there and use it to shape, as *individuals*, life in their public communities. That remains, I believe, the surest hope for the well-being of every religion in this country, as well as for each individual and his or her personal conscience.

8

MIDGE DECTER

MANY years ago, someone complained to the then British prime minister, Sir Harold Macmillan, that the people of Britain had lost their sense of purpose. "If they want a sense of purpose," he replied, "let them go to their bishops."

This was a deeply civilized thing to say—he was a deeply civilized man—and a response whose appositeness it seems not too snooty to suppose few of his interlocutors were likely to have understood. There would be even fewer among us today, when every *i* and *t* in the realm of the spirit must be legalistically dotted and crossed, every apprehension converted to a proposition, every tacit understanding translated to a slogan scrawled on public walls. This is a time, to name but one example, when the iron-and-gossamer connection of husband to wife and of both to child has been turned into something called "family values" and is thus both coarsened and weakened. In the same way, to be forced, as we unquestionably now are, to make a topic of public discussion of the relation between church and state means precisely that we are members of a society that has lost its hold—Harold Macmillan's hold—on the meaning of both.

As for my thinking on this subject, it has not changed; it has only just, haltingly, begun. What should be the role of religion in American public life? Why, to keep us humble, to keep us mindful that we are not a better people than God's other children but are beyond any measure luckier, and perhaps above all to instruct the

Midge Decter is a Fellow of the Institute on Religion and Public Life.

citizens of a democracy where, beyond state and government and policy-making, the true transcendence that every one of us at least sometimes seeks is to be found.

But this is a far cry indeed from the public controversies that our current epidemic of so-called realist atheism has given rise to, such as whether it is permissible to pray or celebrate Christmas in schools and other public institutions, or to grant government support of one kind or another to private religious education. What to do about these? I wish I knew. Not as a Jew—that's easy: whatever unease Jews felt in an American culture dominated by Christianity ain't nothin' compared with the anxiety in store for Jews and everybody else in a culture dominated by ravening atheists (sometimes mistakenly called "humanists"), including, be it noted, for the atheists themselves. Still, it is not easy as an American to know how far we may go before we damage the pluralism that is essential to the special nature of this society, where we are to draw the outer boundaries, and how we are to furnish our desperately naked public square.

But would not God himself enjoin us to be modest and even a little fearful in our deliberations about how best to go about beseeching him to restore our sense of purpose?

9

DONNA ROBINSON DIVINE

IN the United States, Jewish identity is distinctly American. Most Jews rearrange their ancient customs in order to fit them into the mores and values of America. America's Jews have not simply crossed a cultural divide to become part of the mainstream—they are hardly aware that such a divide exists.

Despite official sensitivity to minorities, there is a dominant culture in America. In public schools the languages of immigrant groups are supplanted. Political institutions imprint upon a heterogeneous society the core values of freedom, tolerance, and participation. To subscribe to America's national creed requires assimilation, a process imparting a common language and reorienting loyalties and affiliations. Social mechanisms foster consensus. Continually running up against the danger of divisiveness, the public domain in America selects only safe differences to accent, bypassing those that may be more important. Living in the warm embrace of America exacts a toll paid in cultural currency.

American values have weakened rather than strengthened traditional Jewish identity. As much as America's principles have secured life and livelihoods, they have imposed a single perspective on religion as if it were universal. The judicial system defines the religious sphere, but in countless ways the school as much as the church or synagogue imparts critical assumptions about what reli-

Donna Robinson Divine is a professor of government at Smith College and co-founder of the college's Program in Jewish Studies. She is completing a book on Palestinian Arab society during the last century of Ottoman rule.

gion is and means. Similarities are emphasized as diverse religious cultures are placed within common categories. In that respect, Jews have ceded the power to conceptualize their own religious tradition to America's public arena.

Jews may have found a comfortable place in American society, but the religious framework of reference in America does not fully accommodate Judaism. Where the American model draws connections, traditional Judaism presupposes distinctions. Implying at once an ethnicity, a tie to a land, and a theology, traditional Judaism contains meanings in excess of the meanings conferred on religion by the American framework.

Jewish religious practices have often been honored in the American public domain, which makes them familiar to non-Jews as well as Jews but often renders them alien to their ancestry. Jewish holidays have been recast and reinterpreted. Consider the Passover Seder. Most American Jews, with or without Jewish spouses, observe Passover and attend a Seder. Many non-Jews also regularly celebrate this holiday by participating in a Seder. The holiday's salience for Americans derives from its passion for freedom rather than the Haggadah's exposition of ritual or its discussions of nationhood and theology. The *New York Times* recently listed restaurants providing kosher and non-kosher Seders as if there were no significant difference.

Growing up in America and attending its public schools, the vast number of Jews, so thoroughly attuned to American values, are hardly struck by the extent to which Judaism has been altered. They have been detached from Jewish history, Jewish traditions, and their own distinctiveness as a community.

Jews must generate their own categories of analysis to understand the world and their place in it. They need categories that both define their traditions more accurately and scrutinize more closely the ways in which they are defined by others. This strategy calls for a shift in how Jews determine what is taken for fact about the role of Judaism and Jewish concerns in public life, whether relating to day-school education, Jewish camps, or ties to Israel.

The familiar disposition of American Jewish organizations to oppose state aid for parochial schools may have been a reasonable response to predicaments of the past, but it has an ambiguous value in current circumstances. Earlier, in America, the old were able to teach the young what it meant to be a Jew, but family as a vehicle for transmitting tradition no longer suffices. Only the curriculum of a day school, steeped in the classic texts and languages of the Jewish people, affords Jews proper access to their own civilization. The emergence of a broad-based system of Jewish day schools supported by Orthodox, Conservative and Reform movements suggests that Jewish organizations are beginning to recognize and redress the negative consequences of public-school education. It may be appropriate and necessary for American Jews and Jewish communal organizations to move even further and advocate public support for private religious education.

Attention to Jewish culture as anterior to American culture is likely to highlight the disjuncture between the two. It may mean that adjustment will be difficult and full integration impossible. Nevertheless, changing the angle of vision is necessary to upholding America's Jewish community. There are ways to knit together antagonistic principles, but not before the real conflicts are clarified. For the sake of Jewish survival, the flow of cultural trade has to change directions. Then the American Jewish community can anticipate a creative future, confronting the complexities of modern civilization and borrowing from the dominant political culture in a way that is consistent with its sustaining principles.

10

LEONID FELDMAN

THE goal of the separationists is to make America more secular. I was born and raised in the most secular society in the twentieth century—the Soviet Union. Together with some 500,000 others, I am a refugee from that goal. We have experienced firsthand what happens to a society totally divorced from God and religious values. For example, I never heard my parents tell political jokes, and they never listened to the Voice of America unless my sister and I were asleep. Our parents were afraid of us. They knew that our secular teachers taught us to inform on our parents if they behaved like "enemies of the people."

Our version of the pledge of allegiance was very much in accordance with the principle of separation between church and state (which was always part of the Soviet constitution). This is what we said every morning in school:

> Glory to the Communist Party of the Soviet Union! Lenin lived, Lenin lives, Lenin will live forever! We live in the most perfect society in the world. . . .

I am frightened by secularism. This century, the most secular one in human history, has produced the Gulag and Auschwitz. It has also produced me—a child spying on his father, who would have been proud to report him to the authorities.

It is well known that there are no true atheists or secularists.

Leonid Feldman is the rabbi of Temple Emanu-El in Palm Beach, Florida. He is a former atheist who became the first Soviet-born Conservative rabbi.

Human beings believe either in God or in gods. The health and the future of any society are determined by the answer to one question: Who is the winner in the war between idolatry and ethical monotheism? American society is in deep trouble. It is now obvious that "value-free" education promotes idol worship. Why is it all right to expose our children to all different "isms" except ethical monotheism or Judaism?

The Master of the world chose the Jewish people as his partners in destroying idolatry. The goal of the Jews is not to pray in the synagogue, nor to wear a yarmulke, nor even to keep kosher. Our mission has always been and still is *tikkun olam*—repairing the world by bringing it to *one* God. We have the obligation to repair America. Yet the organized Jewish community is obsessed with removing *one* God from our society. The indirect result of it is promotion of idolatry in America, and the further decline of religion will eventually destroy this country.

The Jewish people used to fight against the pagans, the Crusaders, the Communists, the Nazis. Today we are fighting against the crèches and Christmas trees.

I fought the KGB for the right to light a menorah. Forgive me if I don't want to eliminate menorahs from America's lawns.

11

ABRAHAM H. FOXMAN

THE problems of Jewish life in this country have been fully documented. The National Jewish Population Study, commissioned by the Council of Jewish Federations, provides some sobering statistics:

- Since 1985, 52 per cent of all marriages of Jewish persons have been intermarriages.
- Nearly three-quarters of all children born to intermarried couples are not raised as Jews.
- In the last six years, the Jewish community lost 210,000 people through conversion to Christianity or other religions while gaining only 185,000 converts to the Jewish faith.
- The number of Americans who identify themselves as even minimally practicing Jews has shrunk to 4.3 million, or about 1.8 per cent of the total population.
- Jewish religious and community institutions at all levels are increasingly challenged to maintain their levels of membership and financial support.

The true picture may not be so dismal. The small but growing return of influential—and previously secular—young people to traditional Jewish observance is one example. Many Jewish communities in the United States are active, thriving, and vital. A

Abraham H. Foxman is national director of the Anti-Defamation League. He is vice president of the American Gathering of Jewish Holocaust Survivors.

massive grass-roots response contributed to the financial success of Operation Exodus. American Jews were fully united behind Israel when it came under assault during the Persian Gulf War.

Nonetheless, certain major problems are deeply rooted and seem to be getting worse. On this, both pessimists and optimists must agree.

Some seek to reverse these trends by calling for more religion, both Jewish and Christian, in American public life. The First Amendment protection of freedom *of* religion, they argue, has been reinterpreted in recent years into a movement to secure freedom *from* religion. In effect, they believe that religion in the home and in the synagogue will be enhanced if it is simultaneously emphasized in the schools and in public places.

We of the Anti-Defamation League reject this argument while sympathizing with the honest motivation that produced it. Public, state-sanctioned religious observance would do little to benefit American Judaism and much to harm American life.

In the 1830s, Alexis de Tocqueville, that most perceptive observer of American life and institutions, wrote that religion flourished in America precisely because it was divorced from government support and political entanglement. He knew that the non-denominational quality of American life should not and could not be confused with secularism. He compared the American experience to that of continental Europe, where state-supported established churches were everywhere in decline. The entanglement of church and state, he concluded, was ultimately destructive to both.

Since Tocqueville's day, the industrial and post-industrial revolutions have given us choices of mobility and lifestyle undreamed of in simpler times. Today people can choose to be affiliated or non-affiliated, to observe or not to observe. Being Jewish today is a matter of choice as much as birth. This presents a set of challenges that cannot be met through simple and external solutions.

Separation of state and religion is one of the cornerstones of democratic pluralism in this country, a pluralism that has made it possible for American Jews to flourish as a distinct community fully engaged in the structure of American society. If religion is to occupy the public square, pluralism will ultimately be pushed out.

If democratic pluralism is eroded, Jews and other religious minorities will suffer.

More public displays of denominational belief, more public prayers, will not result in more observant, affiliated, or sincere Jews but will only marginalize us, pushing us away from the center of social and political life. Those who believe every public crèche can be balanced with a public menorah are as naïve as they are wrongheaded.

It is true that the ghetto was a world of deep and meaningful Jewish observance and spirituality. It was also a world of squalor, of physical and moral degradation. We should remember that it was the *internal* strength that sustained our Jewish faith and eventually made possible our involvement in the affairs of the wider world.

The Jewish community in America has real problems. They are both internal and external. ADL's annual *Audit of Anti-Semitic Incidents* for 1991, for instance, showed an 11 per cent increase over 1990 in acts of vandalism, harassment, assaults, and threats against Jews or Jewish institutions. Anti-Semitic attacks on U.S. campuses increased 32 per cent over the past two years.

These problems will require all of our ingenuity, commitment, and compassion. They are not amenable to external quick fixes, especially those that threaten to undermine the very basis of our democratic protections. The battle for Judaism must be fought in our hearts, our homes, our synagogues, and our community institutions. It cannot and should not be conducted in our schools or our streets, or in the halls of government.

12

MURRAY FRIEDMAN

J EWS are political liberals almost by definition. All the public-opinion polls bear this out. Almost alone among white groups in the country throughout the Nixon-Reagan-Bush years, we have clung stubbornly to Democratic presidential candidates.

Jews demonstrate a willingness not only to back liberal candidates but also to support, more than other citizens, governmental efforts to deal with urban problems, improve education, and ensure equal rights for all our citizens. We pride ourselves on being on the side of the poor even though many of us have moved up in this society and lengthened our distance from them.

Yet on an exciting idea that embodies most of the elements in Jewish liberalism—the issue of choice in education, pushed by President Bush on a national level and by a number of activists on a state level—most Jewish religious and civic bodies either are dragging their feet or have in fact opposed this approach to the crisis in urban education.

Choice in education seeks to make it possible for poor and working-class parents, both white and black, to take their children out of failure-prone and crime-ridden public schools and send them to schools where they are likely to receive a better education. Critics

---

Murray Friedman is Middle States director of the American Jewish Committee, in Philadelphia, and director of the Center for the Study of American Jewish History, Temple University. (The views expressed here are not necessarily the views of these organizations.) He is the author of *The Utopian Dilemma: American Judaism and Public Policy* (Ethics and Public Policy Center, 1985).

49

are worried that this would skim off the cream from inner-city schools and leave those who remain locked into even worse situations. There is a legitimate fear that widespread use of vouchers would destroy public schools, which many Jews remember fondly as their launching pad in this society.

These are serious challenges and worthy of debate. But I sense little desire on the part of Jewish leaders to enter into such debate. Instead, we seem to be clinging to a body of clichés and out-of-date information.

The standard position is, "Let them use the money that would go into vouchers to improve the public schools." A second point often made is that public schools provide the greatest opportunity for persons of different religious and racial backgrounds to come together, hence creating a more integrated society. (Of course, in recent years Jews themselves have been abandoning the public schools for private schools in droves, or have moved to the suburbs where they receive, in effect, private education at public expense.)

But what appears to be the greatest sticking point for most Jews is that the vouchers presently projected often provide, as in proposed Pennsylvania legislation, aid to parochial schools, particularly Catholic schools. This is seen as a violation of the constitutional separation of church and state. Many Jews, their nerve endings rubbed raw by the history of ill treatment of Jews in church-dominated societies (both Protestant and Catholic), have opted for buttressing Jefferson's "wall of separation" between religion and public institutions.

Here, then, is the classic conflict between the Jewish desire to stand on the side of social justice and the historic fear that when church and state get too close, it is almost always dangerous, not to say damaging, for Jews. But as we move toward the close of the twentieth century, we need to disenthrall ourselves from some of these historic fears in order to achieve social objectives.

It is difficult for Jews, just a bit more than two generations away from the opening of Hitler's death camps, to make this leap. The Scud missiles plowing into Tel Aviv during the Persian Gulf War only reinforced the feeling that there is a dangerous world out there and we have to be cautious about the "truths" we have learned over the years. Yet the long and proud Jewish tradition of seeking to ameliorate society's ills requires us to update our traditional liberalism, including the church-state bugaboo.

In the past we pressed for school desegregation in part to equalize educational opportunities. Similarly, we now need to give the poor and disadvantaged students a chance to equalize their opportunities.

Even on the matter of integration, Thomas Vitulo Martin has shown that many private schools are more integrated than the public schools in their cities. In 1979, in an essay in the volume *New Perspectives on School Integration*, he pointed out that the Catholic system was 18 per cent minority and that this percentage was increasing. The minority percentage was particularly high in some dioceses. Catholic schools in the Montgomery district of the Mobile, Alabama, diocese were 63 per cent black. Schools of the Birmingham diocese, which includes all of northern Alabama, were 43 per cent black. The Catholic elementary schools of the District of Columbia were 77 per cent minority. They are even more integrated today.

As liberals concerned with making America's cities more viable, Jews have another reason to favor the preserving of parochial schools. These schools and the parishes that operate them are anchors for holding working-class whites in the cities. If the schools disappear, more of this segment of the population will abandon the cities, leaving these neighborhoods and the public schools more isolated and desolate than before.

There is even a direct Jewish stake involved here. Large numbers of Jewish children are attending day schools where their Jewishness is enhanced as they develop civic and personal skills. The costs of running these schools have grown enormously. The argument against "double taxation"—parents forced by religious belief and tradition to support religious schools while paying for the cost of public education as well—seems to look better and better. In effect, Jewish education, so necessary for Jewish survival, is available mainly for the well-to-do. Educational vouchers can be one small piece of the Jewish struggle for survival in our society today.

There is finally—let us face this matter openly—the historic Jewish fear of Roman Catholics, based on our difficult interaction down through the years. Whatever it may have been in the past and elsewhere in the world, the Catholic Church in America has become part and parcel of a democratic society. The evidence is abundantly at hand. At the Second Vatican Council the American hierarchy fought for and won the historic *Nostra Aetate* declaration, which redefined attitudes of the Catholic Church towards Jews. Studies by Andrew Greeley, Joseph Fichter, and others make it clear that parochial schools teach the democratic idea and ideals of the society. And I know of no institution, including the public schools, that has taken the Holocaust in Europe during World War II so much to heart and that teaches its important lessons so assiduously to its children as the Catholic parochial schools. To the degree that they educate children for their role as citizens in our society, parochial schools need our help.

There is reason to believe that there will be no progress in urban education unless we create new opportunities for our poor and working classes as well as for Roman Catholics, whose private schools represent the largest grouping in private education. Can Jews move out from a body of ideas that fit an earlier period and adjust them to the needs of a modern society?

13

MARC GELLMAN

M Y thinking about the role of religion in public life has been influenced by wildly different forces.

First there was the Vietnam War and the *Kulturkampf* it unleashed in America, which released me from an undifferentiated Milwaukee childhood into the late-1960s stampede of many Americans to find an alternative identity that was not primarily American, with all the ugly imperialistic resonances and responsibilities the name implied. With America seen as a global oppressor, I sought refuge in my Jewish identity. The comforting and conveniently guilt-free identity of the Jew as victim was, in my mind at least, immune to the facts of Jewish power and acceptance in America. In that guilt-ridden time I needed to cloak myself in the moral innocence of a victim. I became a Jewish-Radical, one of the many hyphenated rebels of that tumultuous time.

The one virtue of this charade was that I came to consciousness believing that my religious identity and my sense of political activism were utterly intertwined. My socialism at the time included more quotations from Isaiah than from Marx, which was fair enough because my Judaism included more quotations from Marx than from Isaiah. However infantile my theology and my political theories may have been, I believed then, and I believe now, that God commands us to speak the truth of our faith both in our home and on our way, both when we lie down and when we rise up. A

Marc Gellman is the rabbi of Temple Beth Torah in Dix Hills, N.Y., and co-author (with Thomas Hartman) of *Where Does God Live?*

religion that does not matter in the streets cannot matter in the pews. I had no real idea at the time how all this played out. I was satisfied simply to trail the Movement, providing biblical and Talmudic quotes to justify what the left was going to do anyway.

I left the left when I perceived it as turning against Israel. What I felt among my comrades was the strong and frankly anti-Semitic impulse to blame Jews once we were no longer victims. Oppressive Arab dictatorships received nothing like the calumny that the left heaped on democratic Israel, and I resented it deeply. I retain my sympathy for the Palestinian people, but I remain unconvinced that a true Palestinian moderate leader can survive and be followed. Clearly it was my Jewish identity that compelled me to alter my political identity. In other times the opposite would no doubt have occurred.

The second blow from the left came when the black-power movement in America turned its back on whites, and with special vitriol on Jews. This was a bitter time for me. My first rabbinic mentor had been fired from his pulpit because he decided to march with Martin Luther King in the South. I felt deeply proud of the Jewish contributions to the civil-rights movement. I considered Michael Schwerner and Andrew Goodman martyrs, not just political victims. My hero, Rabbi Abraham Joshua Heschel, marched with King in Selma not as a token Jew but as a trusted partner in the struggle.

The civil-rights movement was for me redolent with religious meaning and metaphor. For me, the Rev. Dr. Martin Luther King was primarily the Reverend, not a Doctor. I felt then and I feel now that it was the power of his faith more than the power of his political ideology that accounted both for his political successes and for his oratorical passion. When the civil-rights movement was taken over by secular black radicals, that religious vision faded and the movement collapsed. It left me with the lesson that a religious vision is essential to overcoming the social ills of America. I believe that the forces of goodness and understanding, of toleration and justice, must rediscover their authentic religious roots before the tree of social justice will again bear fruit.

Then I began to think about fetuses. I thought about them first in the context of my doctoral dissertation in philosophy, and later as a Jew and as a recovering American. To my amazement, the more I thought about it the more I realized that my liberal and radical friends had gotten the abortion thing all wrong.

This struggle for a woman's right to have an abortion when the pregnancy does not threaten her life or her health does not feel like the struggle to get Rosa Parks a place on the Montgomery bus or James Meredith a place in the University of Mississippi. Those struggles were imbued with the aroma of justice overcoming bigotry. This struggle smells like a fight to keep women and men from accepting the consequences of sexual promiscuity. How narrow and selfish that seems to me now.

I was bewildered by the inability of so many of my Movement friends to translate their compassion and peacefulness, their regard for life and health, into compassion for fetuses, who, despite their disputed moral status before birth, would eventually become persons with the right to find a life for themselves.

I suspected that the primary reason for the left's blindness on abortion was the instinctive cultural disdain felt for pro-life advocates. They listened to Lawrence Welk, not the Grateful Dead; they had purple hair and white sequined glasses, not long hair and wire-rimmed glasses. They were the ones we had seen across the picket lines in Selma. But on this issue they somehow got it right and we got it wrong. It did not escape my notice that many of the pro-life people were moved by their faith to take this position. I could not say that about the pro-choice people I knew. The pro-life people spoke of rights and wrongs, while the pro-choice people spoke of rights and laws. The former language was far more congenial to me personally, and far closer to my sense of how God wants us to make religion real in the world.

I found that, absent a clear threat to the life of the mother, I could no longer condone the killing of fetuses. In consulting my faith and its rich legal traditions, I found that my thinking was much in line with orthodox Jewish law on the morality of abortion. Though Jewish law is relatively clear in not considering the fetus a bearer of moral rights, it is equally clear in prohibiting abortion save to protect the life or basic health of the mother.

Never did it occur to me that Judaism's opposition to elective abortions should be considered an inappropriate reason to be pro-life. Never did I think that the separation doctrine of the Constitution prohibited my Judaism from informing my moral choices and from motivating me to work to see those choices made real in the marketplace of ideas that shapes public policy. I had never apologized for being pro–civil rights on the basis of the Bible; why should I apologize for being pro-life on the basis of the Talmud?

What I concluded was that there was bad faith here on the part of pro-choice people who, because they disagreed with the conclusions of religiously motivated pro-life people, disparaged the religious motivations that undergirded them. There was no such uproar about the Reverend Dr. King's religious motivations for civil rights; they were a part of making civil rights a holy crusade.

I see no reason why religious Americans should feel hesitant to express their religious views and to urge that those views become public policy. I am still uncertain about how my view on abortion ought to be translated, if at all, into public policy, but I know that the killing of a fetus is not a morally neutral act that ought to be covered by some privacy doctrine, whether invented or discovered in the Constitution.

God is not finished with me, but I know now that the Judaism that has been with me since I came to maturity speaks, not only in the room where I light shabbat candles, but also and essentially to the world that shivers outside the glow of those candles.

14

DAVID M. GORDIS

I belong to the majority of Jews in America, those who have been strongly committed to the separation of church and state and have generally supported the separationist position in matters of school prayer, equal access, and public display of religious symbols. I have been uneasy with the view of many that this position suggests a lack of concern over the deterioration of public and personal ethics in this country. I reject the assertion that public-policy debates should be uninformed by concern for values. As a religious person, I am committed to a religion that is concerned with social realities and seeks to influence society's ethical standards and behavior. What appears to some to be an inconsistency, namely, asserting a greater social role for religion while affirming separationism, suggests the need to articulate a distinction that seems almost self-evident but apparently is not: the distinction between "church and state" issues and "religion and society" issues.

"Religion and society" issues have to do with the ways religion functions in the world. Should religiously rooted perspectives be introduced into discussions of public-policy matters? If theologically linked views are to be included in debates over social-ethical issues, should the theological language in which they are expressed be translated into a more generally appealing form of discourse, not to conceal their origins but to make them persuasive to those

David M. Gordis is president of Hebrew College in Boston and director of the Wilstein Institute of Jewish Policy Studies. He is a rabbi and holds a Ph.D. in Talmud.

who do not adhere to the theology they represent? "Religion and society" issues include questions of the visibility and audibility of religious figures in public-policy deliberations, both in matters of direct concern to religious groups and in broader areas of ethics, social purpose, political philosophy, and social responsibility.

"Church and state" issues are far more limited. They relate to the specific modes of relationship between organized religion and the legal and political structures of society. While avowed secularists view the separation of church and state as a protection against the influence of religion on public life, the separationist position does not necessarily imply the further purpose of excluding religion from the public sphere. I, for example, am a separationist but not a secularist. The assertion that separation has been good for both religion and government remains persuasive even for someone such as myself who is sympathetic to the critics of the "naked public square" and who would urge a greater voice for religion in American public life. In my view, neither public display of crèches or Hanukkah menorahs nor prayer in the public schools is a serious way to deal with the problem of social discourse and policy deliberation that takes no account of the ethical implications of the positions advocated. Concern with a public forum empty of value concerns does not imply the advocacy of a wholesale breakdown of the pattern of separation, a pattern that in many ways has served our country's religious and political structures well.

Binary approaches to complex issues impede rather than nurture communication. The *First Things* symposium that led to the writing of this essay, and the very phenomenon of *First Things*, will, I hope, help overcome rather than sustain a binary approach to issues of religion and society in the Jewish community. Just as the critics of the naked public square deserve to be heard by the separationists, so do the separationists deserve to be listened to more carefully by those who propose attenuation of the existing patterns of separation. If Jewish and Christian symbols are to be sanctioned in public places, how do we protect the minority religious groups that form major strands in the tapestry of American life? Does the public elementary school become a marketplace for missionary activity of all sorts in the wake of equal-access legislation? *Whose* prayer in the schools? And what does any of this have to do with a really constructive response to the pathologies confronting us in our cities, in our families, and in the individual lives of so many?

We need to move beyond the bashing of villains on the right or on the left, beyond superficial responses to the profound aridity of public life, and find ways that can relieve that aridity without creating more problems than they solve. There is need to encourage more of the kind of thinking that is reflected in *First Things*, from a range of political perspectives. The work of the U.S. Catholic bishops on matters of economic concern and on war-and-peace issues, as well as the reactions to that work, is important and constructive and deserves to be emulated by other religious groups. The Wilstein Institute of Jewish Policy Studies (which I direct) is engaged in such efforts.

Religious figures should be seen and heard on issues of social ethics and public policy; but when they speak outside the ecclesiastical setting and to those outside their own religious constituencies they should be encouraged to speak, not *ex cathedra*, but rather in the language and style of public deliberation, open to debate and refutation. More imaginative work needs to be done on teaching values in the schools and on finding ways to overcome the impression that religion is insignificant or even pernicious, an impression created by the absence of religion from the public-school curriculum. We should bear in mind, however, that to attribute any particular political view to the Divine is likely to display not piety but religious arrogance.

In dealing with matters of such weight, it is useful to remember that we are engaged in the American *experiment*. We are reflecting together upon patterns that have evolved in this country over the course of twelve generations, and we are seeking ways to refine these patterns. Our way of dealing with matters of religion and society is the product of our constitutional foundation, deliberations by Americans throughout our history on the best way to articulate that constitutional vision in the social reality, and a constantly evolving perspective on how best to achieve desirable social ends within that framework. It is best that we pursue whatever adjustments we ultimately deem useful with respect and reverence for what has preceded our efforts. This will help us move forward in an appropriate spirit: modesty concerning our own capacities, and faith that the positions we put forward will be part of the solution, not the problem.

15

JOSHUA O. HABERMAN

As a former liberal who turned conservative, I have changed my mind on a number of questions of public policy, but not on the separation of church and state. I believe that this principle is as sound as ever and beneficial to both religion and the state.

This is not to say that I am satisfied with the moral and spiritual condition of America. I am appalled by the apparent moral decay, the falling apart of the family, and the neo-pagan hedonism that expresses itself, in its mildest form, in narcissistic body culture and, more harmfully, in sexual promiscuity, alcoholism, and drug addiction. For all this I do not blame the government, Congress, legislation, or church-state relations but the state of mind of the American people.

The problem is in the corruption of our culture, the erosion of the *sancta*, that mixture of beliefs and morals that is the heart of civilization. This erosion, which in the course of several centuries brought Europe to the cynical amoralism and nihilism of the pre–World War II days, is now evident in America. That it may undo us at a much faster pace is suggested by the decline of honesty, of education, and of work and business ethics, and the rise in virtually every kind of crime.

I believe that the remedy lies in a moral turnabout as part of a spiritual renewal that should be the agenda of religion. If it isn't

Joshua O. Haberman is president of the Foundation for Jewish Studies and adjunct professor at Wesley Theological Seminary, Washington, D.C. He is rabbi emeritus of the Washington Hebrew Congregation.

happening, the fault is not in the strict application of the principle of church-state separation but in the quality of religious leadership. Religion in America right now has more exposure, more access to public life and influence than it knows how to use effectively. With few exceptions, churches and synagogues are themselves riding the crest of secularization and falling in line with cultural fads. All too easily they surrender their moral patrimony to the neo-pagan revolt that is called "the new morality."

Churches and synagogues must stop trying to be all things to all people. Priests, ministers, and rabbis must stop being jacks-of-all-trades, or just "nice guys" who, in order to be liked, try to be like everyone else, and cater to all kinds of needs and interests that are irrelevant to their central task as spiritual leaders. Their all-consuming job must be to teach and preach principles of faith and morals so as to affect the state of mind of their people and fortify them religiously.

I am for strict separation of church and state in America. As a conservative I believe in keeping government out of my hair as much as possible. I want greater privatization in various economic sectors, in education, and in cultural life. I view with apprehension the growing control of our entire health-care system by the state. By the same token, I am deeply suspicious of all proposals that would bring religion and various state agencies into some sort of "partnership" and entrust certain religious functions to publicly funded institutions and their religiously unqualified staffs. The crucial battle of religion is to be fought not in the public square but in the minds of the people. I see no help for the cause of religion in religious flag-waving, in the public display of religious symbols, in routinized school prayers, or in those hurried salutes to God at the opening of public assemblies.

In one area of major contention in church-state relations, however, I have changed my mind. I used to oppose parochial schools; I now favor them. I strongly believe in maintaining parents' control over their children's education. I favor the educational voucher plan. Its absence robs parents of their option in their children's education. For parents to pay the cost of private education in addition to taxes for public schools is unfair. I also believe all other auxiliary services such as bus transportation, school lunches, medical services, and textbooks should be available to public-school and parochial-school children alike. I regard this kind of financial aid to parochial schools not as state support for religion but a matter of equity in the allocation of tax money.

No wiser words were ever spoken about the role of religion in American life than Alexis de Tocqueville's comments in his *Democracy in America* (1839). Religion, he observed, has two supremely important functions in America. First, it builds the consensus for inner moral restraints that are all the more necessary when democracy relaxes external control over the lives of its citizens. Secondly, religion upholds first principles of beliefs and moral mandates derived from a transcendent authority that sets limits to governmental power. These absolutes, anchored in the conscience of the faithful, cannot be set aside by legislation or governmental decree. They represent the ultimate ground of our basic human rights.

These two functions of religion in American life can best be carried out by religious leaders who, in total independence from the state, are free to speak *to* the state under a mandate from authority above the state. It is therefore entirely in the interest of religion that I wish to maintain the strict separation of church and state.

Having reaffirmed this principle, I urge that we not make a fetish of it or lose all sense in applying it. Mark Twain told about a cat who jumped on a hot stove, got burned, and rightly learned the lesson not to sit on a hot stove, but carried the lesson to excess by refusing to sit on a cold stove. The memory of the European experience of religious wars and persecutions that inspired our American doctrine of the separation of church and state must not be carried to excess. We must not become paranoid about any and all relationships between public policy and religion in America.

If the state is to be neutral on religion, its neutrality should be a benevolent one, not a spiteful or hostile aloofness. For example, if religious practices are inappropriate in the public school, this should not lead to the banishment of all religious data from the school curriculum. The history, the contribution, and the present role of religion, in the world and in American life particularly, should be fully recognized in the teaching of history, literature, and the arts. Such curricula should be developed in consultation with the best qualified representatives of the various religious bodies and with the advice of a major inter-religious forum or organization, yet to be created, that can define the common moral and spiritual ground of all the major religious bodies in America.

16

MILTON HIMMELFARB

IT has been said before and needs to be said again: The trouble is not that religion in general has too small a role in American public life. The trouble is that a particular religion has too great a role—paganism, the *de facto* established religion. When dissenters argue that it is no business of government to endow Robert Mapplethorpe's paganism, the "arts community" and its friends raise an alarm about bigoted philistines.

Let historicists wince at statements that begin, "Judaism is. . . ." Judaism is against paganism.

Hayyehudi, "the Jew," occurs six times in Scripture, always in apposition to "Mordecai": "Mordecai the Jew." (He is also once called "a Jew" and once "a Jewish man.") In Rabbi Johanan's exegesis (Megillah 13a), Mordecai is called Jew so insistently because he abjured paganism ['*avodah zarah*]. "For everyone who abjures paganism is called a Jew; as is written (Daniel 3:12): ". . . Jews . . . serve not thy gods nor worship the golden image which thou hast set up."

From the beginning, Judaism has equated paganism and unchastity. Leviticus 18 forbids Israel the Egyptian and Canaanite pagans' unchaste laws (*huqqot*): biblically, unchastity is not an option for pagans but a requirement. "Rabbi Judah said, citing Rav: 'Israel [in the backsliding days of the First Temple] knew that paganism has

Milton Himmelfarb is a former editor of the *American Jewish Year Book* and a former contributing editor of *Commentary*. He is the author of *The Jews of Modernity* (Basic Books, 1973).

no substance. They professed paganism only to indulge in flagrant debauchery' " (Sanhedrin 63b). Orthodox and Conservative congregations read Leviticus 18 on Yom Kippur.

It could have been in Queen Victoria's reign that Reform, worrying like Mr. Podsnap about bringing a blush to the cheek of the young person, banished Leviticus 18 in favor of selected verses from 19. The windfall now for a devoutly advanced rabbinate is that members of Reform congregations need never hear Leviticus 18:22.

The first volume of the historian Peter Gay's *Enlightenment* is subtitled, in part, *The Rise of Modern Paganism*. The Enlightenment's project was liberal—to liberate us for the pursuit of our happiness. But much of what began as liberal has turned libertine, and libertinism has brought not liberation and happiness so much as enslavement and misery: AIDS, kids who have kids, the absent father. First the French Revolution devoured its children, then the Bolshevik Revolution, and now the sexual revolution.

Drugs, too, are a pagan devourer. In paganism you own your body, and you are as free to ruin it as to ruin any other property of yours. In Judaism you are no more free to harm yourself than to harm another.

With less paganism and less of its bitter fruit, America would be less diseased, fear-ridden, ignorant, poor. Surely American Jewry will do what is necessary to help bring this about?

As the Duke of Wellington said about something else: If you can believe that, you can believe anything. Paganism? That's so—so *fundamentalist*, so *right-wing*.

During the Mapplethorpe affair the *New York Times* decreed a governmental duty to endow exhibits that "documented a sadomasochistic homosexual subculture." The *Times* has yet to instruct us about a duty to endow exhibits documenting—celebrating?—other sadomasochistic subcultures.

In Cincinnati a curator had to defend in court his museum's way of championing Art against its enemies, which was to exhibit the Mapplethorpe collection. (He was acquitted, the jury deferring to its betters about "What Is Art?") One expert witness for the defense testified that the photograph of a penis with inserted finger was "a very ordered, classical composition," and that the photograph of an arm in an anus was formally similar to the photograph of a flower.

In the opinion of the *Times*'s photography editor, the curator of a university museum "came closest to the truth when she told the prosecutor . . . , 'It's the tension between the physical beauty of the photograph and the brutal nature of what's going on in it that gives it the particular quality that this work of art has.' "

She was not asked about a hypothetically beautiful photograph of what was going on in a Nazi torture chamber.

When the esthetic and the ethical conflict, paganism sides with the esthetic and Judaism with the ethical. In the nineteenth century, Matthew Arnold's Hellenism/Hebraism and Samuel David Luzzato's Atticism/Abrahamism drew that distinction. (In the twelfth century, Judah Ha-levi's *Kuzari* drew it.) Arnold thought that Victorian Hebraism pressed too hard on Hellenism. Though in our day the effortless low paganism that ousted his kind of Hellenism presses much harder on Hebraism, most American Jews do not champion Hebraism in its distress. They champion separationism, separation of church and state as an absolute. But separationism favors paganism, if only because paganism is not a generally recognized religion. It is merely the dominant outlook, the informing spirit of the times.

To the backward who say that a Christ-in-urine is not the sort of thing that government should endow, the Establishment responds that denying a grant would be, *horribile dictu*, censorship. Besides, the money given to that brave artist was only a tiny fraction of the Arts budget.

If, implausibly, the same tiny fraction went to art for a church or synagogue, the *Times* and its clones would thunder against that unforgivable breach in the Wall of Separation. Whether the money was much or little would not matter—principle would be at stake. The money would have to be returned, the guilty punished, watch-dogs posted.

It has been a long time since I began to criticize the separationist dogma of American Jews, and I have since come to think of these separationists as diehard conservatives. With our eyes we have seen the unimaginable become miraculously actual: resurgent Israel, Leningrad once again St. Petersburg, the conquering religion of

Communism a memory. Everything has changed, but American Jews have not changed.

British Jews, who do not shudder at a Chief Rabbi in the House of Lords, are always puzzled by the fuss they think American Jews make about separation. In France and its Jewish community, separationism used to be even more deeply rooted than it is here; but a Chief Rabbi of France once told me how disappointed he was to find American Jews still so separationist. In substance he said: "Don't they realize how that has fostered irreligion"—he meant paganism—"and how that in turn has fostered crime and every other evil? In France we realize it now." (I remember noting that he was not Ashkenazi.)

Tiqqun means "setting right, repairing, correcting, perfecting." Jews on the left who like to give a Jewish cast to their politics have hijacked the tradition's *tiqqun 'olam*, "setting the world right," and made it mean whatever is currently on the left's agenda.

In the tradition itself the *'Alenu* prayer (which Solomon Schecter called the Jewish "Marseillaise") has this: ". . . in hope we wait, O Lord our God, for the idols to be removed from the earth. . . *letaggen 'olam bemalkhut Shaddai* the world being set right by the kingship of the Almighty. . . ." The prayer ends with two verses: "The LORD shall reign for ever and ever" (Exodus 15:18) and ". . . the LORD shall be king over all the earth: in that day shall there be one LORD and his name one" (Zechariah 14:9). *Tiqqun 'olam* is *tiqqun* from paganism.

Will the Synagogue Council, the National Jewish Community Relations Advisory Council, ADL, or either of the AJCs appoint a Task Force on Combatting Paganism? We should live so long.

On the other hand, hope and trust are Jewish virtues. We have seen miracles weightier still.

17

JON D. LEVENSON

> The Government of the United States, which gives to bigotry no sanction, to persecution no assistance, requires only that they who live under its protection should demean themselves as good citizens, in giving it on all occasions their effectual support.

THESE words of George Washington to the Hebrew Congregation of Newport, Rhode Island, articulated the basis of a radically new situation in human history: Jews and Christians as full and equal citizens under a government neutral between the two great traditions. The new arrangement would soon be raised to the level of a fundamental right in the very first stipulation of the First Amendment to the Constitution of the United States: "Congress shall make no law respecting an establishment of religion, or prohibiting the free exercise thereof." In light of the history of bigotry and persecution that has been a central feature of Jewish experience from late biblical times on and to which Washington made tasteful allusion, it is hardly surprising that Jews have been among the most uncompromising supporters of the separation of religion and state. Erosion of the principle would bode ill for Jews and Judaism.

The Founding Fathers are not well served, however, if the impression is left that they thought the new arrangement could also

Jon D. Levenson is the Albert A. List Professor of Jewish Studies in the Divinity School and the Department of Near Eastern Languages and Civilizations at Harvard University. He is author of *Sinai and Zion: An Entry into the Jewish Bible* and *Creation and Persistence of Evil: The Jewish Drama of Divine Omnipotence.*

be neutral between religion and secularity. "Where is the security for property, for reputation, for life," asked Washington in his Farewell Address, "if the sense of religious obligation *desert* the oaths which are the instruments of investigation in courts of justice?" "Reason and experience," he solemnly warned, "both forbid us to expect that national morality can prevail in exclusion of religious principle." Thomas Jefferson, one of the staunchest disestablishmentarians and free-thinkers among the Founders, gave even more pointed expression to the theological foundation of the new republic:

> And can the liberties of a nation be thought secure when we have removed their only firm basis, a conviction in the minds of the people that these liberties are the gift of God? That they are not to be violated but with his wrath? Indeed I tremble for my country when I reflect that God is just.

What the Founders generally desired was a system of government that would respect the authority and justice of God while refraining from endorsing the claims to revelation of any given religious tradition.

The Founders were keenly aware of the exceedingly demanding set of virtues necessary if their experiment in republican government was to endure. These virtues included concern for the common good, love of liberty, reverence for law, responsiveness to duty, respect for property, self-control, moderation, and frugality. Why they did not establish a mechanism to inculcate these essential habits of character, along with reverence for God, in the citizenry of the new republic is easily explained. Most of these virtues had always been prominent in Christianity (and Judaism as well), and they would be acquired more effectively and economically in the home and the local community than through any initiatives of the modest government that the Founding Fathers set up.

The modesty of government is one of the features of American culture in the period of the early republic that are long since gone. The decades since World War II have witnessed an exponential increase in the size of the state; even in what is now misleadingly termed the "private sector," institutions and ways of thinking are shaped or reshaped by government in innumerable ways, great and small. Furthermore, the state has become so secular that the "exclusion of religious principle" against which Washington solemnly warned has become one of the hallmarks of policies formulated in the city that bears his name. Education, though today vastly more available than in earlier times, has been progressively bled not only of religion but of morality as well. In many American classrooms at every level of instruction, the republican virtues esteemed by the Founders are now more likely to be deconstructed than inculcated.

The rates of violent crime, abortion, substance abuse, sexual promiscuity, divorce, conspicuous consumption, and unethical litigation, which have also increased exponentially in recent decades, suggest that Washington's and Jefferson's worries about secularization warrant reconsideration. Although participation in a religious community provides no immunity to these familiar malignancies, there is reason to suspect that their phenomenal spread is not unrelated to the increasing dominance of the secular sector over the rest of society. Need it be mentioned that a society defenseless against its own moral breakdown is unlikely to remain an environment in which Jews can continue to dwell in safety and dignity?

The proper course lies, not in a diminishment of the Establishment Clause of the First Amendment, but in a more vigilant application of the Free Exercise Clause. Nothing of substance will be gained from over-symbolic moves, like setting up crèches and menorahs in front of City Hall or reintroducing prayer in public schools. (And which prayers would be used? The rosary? Something from the Qur'an? "Our Father Who Art in Heaven," which is ascribed to Jesus? A New Age liturgy?) Instead, ways must be found to re-empower the communities of memory and mutual care that mediate between the state and the individual. This, in turn, entails the nearly revolutionary step of disestablishing secularism: the prejudicial notion that religious communities are an exception to the public order rather than full-fledged participants in it must be given up, as must policies based upon this wrong-headed idea.

For example, those who wish their children to be educated in their tradition (whatever it be) must no longer be required to pay twice, once for public schools committed to secularism and once for their private institutions. In the present circumstances, some variety of voucher system is imperative if the Free Exercise Clause is to be honored as it deserves. And need it be mentioned that the future of the Jews is imperiled in any society that, in effect, imposes a fine on those who enable their children to fulfill one of the most basic obligations in Judaism: to serve the God of Israel by studying his Torah daily, extensively, and in depth?

18

SANFORD LEVINSON

To ask what role religion ought to play in American public life raises a variety of questions. As a law professor I am immediately reminded of controversies swirling around the Establishment Clause of the First Amendment, but my views are shaped by far more than formal legal study.

I grew up in the late 1940s and '50s as a member of a distinctly minority Jewish population in a small North Carolina town. The state gave me, at the conclusion of the third grade, a Bible certificate for memorizing Bible verses—including John 3:16. Every December, my grammar school marched *en masse* to the local Methodist church to sing Christmas carols. (I sang all the words except "Christ our Lord" and the like.) I support completely the removal from our public schools of this kind of Christian indoctrination—whether prayers, Bible verses, or Christmas carols. (I am no happier, incidentally, if the prayers are "Jewish"; I rejoice in the recent decision rejecting the constitutionality of prayers during a graduation ceremony, even though the prayer in that case was given by a rabbi.)

Needless to say, I find wholly unprincipled the Supreme Court's decisions upholding Nebraska's right to pay public monies for a legislative chaplain and allowing state sponsorship of Christmas crèches and Hanukkah menorahs. Indeed, I would strip "In God

Sanford Levinson holds the W. St. John Garwood and W. St. John Garwood, Jr., Regents Chair in Law at the University of Texas Law School. He is the author of *Constitutional Faith* (Princeton, 1988).

We Trust" from our currency and "under God" from the pledge of allegiance. It is no part of the state's prerogative to enunciate a theology or to make religious declarations on behalf of its citizenry (or, as in the graduation ceremony, to impose sitting through a prayer as the price of attending a public event).

But I also am opposed to treating the religious *less* well than the non-religious. Separation does not entail hostility. Thus I supported the recent law granting access to public-school facilities for religious groups on equal terms with non-religious groups like the chess and French clubs. Similarly, if the state allows secular groups to present programs in public parks and the like, it must give religious groups the same rights. I can even live with, though I do not support, "moment of silence" laws that allow children to begin the school day with a moment of quiet contemplation during which some will undoubtedly pray. (I agree with the Supreme Court, though, that the state should in no way *encourage* children to pray.)

These represent fairly long-settled views. But I *have* substantially changed my mind on an extremely important issue involving religion and public life: funding of religion-related schools. Having long agreed with my ACLU colleagues that all such aid was unconstitutional (and certainly wrong as a matter of public policy), I have reversed my position. The goad was a brilliant article by conservative University of Chicago law professor Michael McConnell ("The Selective Funding Problem: Abortions in Religious Schools," published in the *Harvard Law Review* in 1991), who began by noting that many liberals support governmental funding of abortions for non-well-off women. We argue that the formal right of every women to enjoy reproductive freedom is hollow if it is rationed by price. McConnell asked liberals a deceptively simple question: If we are so solicitous about ensuring the practical right of poor women to enjoy their right of reproductive choice, why not be equally concerned about the constitutionally protected right of less-well-off parents to choose religious education for their children?

The Supreme Court has held that the Constitution protects the right of parents to choose private education for their children, and the appeal of such a right is obviously strongest when it is connected to the altogether plausible belief that non-public education is an important part of maintaining a child's religious identity. Many parents simply cannot afford non-public education, in part, of course, because taxes for public education continue to mount. I believe that the state may choose to return some of this tax money through support for non-public education. Otherwise, only the well-off would, practically, be guaranteed their constitutional rights, and I find that objectionable on egalitarian grounds.

One could, of course, satisfy the egalitarian rationale by opposing *all* non-public education, and I have been tempted by such a view. But it is ultimately unacceptable. If one genuinely supports pluralism, diversity, and multiculturalism, then one cannot be indifferent to the fact that such a society is possible only when each group has a genuine ability to maintain itself. Indeed, it is worth recalling that much of American hostility to aid to religious schools is the enduring legacy of Protestant antagonism to the maintenance of a flourishing Roman Catholic immigrant culture.

There is a far broader question about which my views are in flux. That is the extent to which explicitly religion-based arguments ought to be welcomed into the public square as part of the general discourse about public policy. On the one hand, it is unfair to tell the religious that they can speak only in the vocabulary of secularists like myself, and any such requirement would be utterly alien to American historical experience. On the other hand, I fear a society in which groups feel little or no duty to present their arguments in a vocabulary that transcends, as much as possible, the strictly sectarian. Still, practically speaking, it is hard to denounce Catholic bishops for using a religious vocabulary to discuss abortion while praising their willingness to criticize the excesses of capitalist materialism or the indecencies of modern warfare. Society may benefit from having within it strong institutions that have transnational loyalties and the psychic capacity to resist the blandishments of the state. Historically, religious institutions have been among the strongest of these.

Finally, I should note that I make my comments within the context of American society and its basic absorption of the important lessons of pluralistic liberalism. In regard to Israel (and to Poland), on the other hand, I am appalled by the complete interpenetration of Judaism and state (and the power lust of the

Catholic Church in Poland) and strongly support a more secularized state. There can be, I believe, no general, acontextual answers
to the questions of religion in public life, for we must be ever
attentive to the particular history and circumstances of the society
under discussion.

19

NATHAN LEWIN

I am proud to be—and always have been—an antidisestablish-mentarianist. In my grade-school days, this was the longest English word we could imagine. No one seemed to know what it meant, and I surely never dreamed I would ever describe myself as one. But that is what I am.

The strict separationists—those who condemn every financial or ceremonial link of government with religion—have succeeded in persuading the courts over the past half-century to dismantle or forbid any church-state association that might be viewed as an "establishment of religion." Their success has, I think, crippled Judaism in the United States. Rather than stimulating Jewish identity, observance, and pride, the national Jewish organizations have promoted Jewish ignorance, indifference, and insecurity by their determined campaign to eliminate religion from public life. It was momentarily satisfying for me to win, in the Supreme Court, against the opposition of the Jewish disestablishmentarianists, the right to display a menorah in front of a city hall. But I recognize that while we prevailed in a small battle, they have won the war.

Twenty years ago, when I wrote the *amicus curiae* brief for the National Jewish Commission on Law and Public Affairs (COLPA) in the Supreme Court in *Lemon* v. *Kurtzman*—the landmark case on aid to parochial schools—I truly believed we could win. We

Nathan Lewin is a Washington attorney who has been a vice president of the National Jewish Commission on Law and Public Affairs (COLPA) since 1969 and has litigated a number of religious-liberty cases in the Supreme Court.

argued a constitutional proposition that seems right to me today: that it is a violation of the Free Exercise Clause of the First Amendment to require religious parents, who are conscientiously bound to send their children to religious schools, to pay taxes for public education (which they cannot use) if their religious schools are not compensated for the cost of teachers in secular programs that are required by state law. I remember my great disappointment in reading Chief Justice Burger's opinion in *Lemon*, but I hoped then that we would, some day, have a Supreme Court majority that would recognize the paramount importance of the Free Exercise Clause.

The current conservative Court majority has taken a different and unexpected tack. Instead of strengthening the Free Exercise Clause and diminishing the Establishment Clause, it has chosen to strangle the former and starve the latter. The Oregon peyote decision (*Employment Division* v. *Smith*, 1990) suddenly eradicated the Free Exercise Clause. With all the advance notice of Pearl Harbor and with no relevant request from any party in the case or from any *amicus*, Justice Antonin Scalia and four of his brethren obliterated the few Supreme Court precedents that protect religious observers and gave lower courts, as well as federal agencies, free rein to override the good-faith claims of religious minorities.

This ominous development heightens the need for Jews to ensure that we and our institutions remain visible. If the Constitution, as currently interpreted, gives the courts no power to guarantee our right to observe our religion, we must be certain that other societal institutions give us latitude and visibility. Jewish adults and children feel they are part of America and its culture when they see a municipality's Hanukkah menorah. A land with so celebrated a tradition of religious diversity may surely signify its respect for the conscientious convictions of its citizens.

Judaism will survive in the United States, notwithstanding the lure of assimilation, if Jewish identity is respected and Jewish learning encouraged. Prohibiting all public acknowledgments of Judaism and barring any possible public benefits to Jewish institutions conveys the wrong message to America's Jews. It tells them to hang, rather than lift, their heads.

20

ALAN MITTLEMAN

THE Zionist thinker Ahad Ha'am distinguished between the "problem of the Jews" and the "problem of Judaism." Political Zionism—the attempt to secure a homeland through diplomatic means for oppressed Jewry—aimed solely, in Ahad Ha'am's view, at a solution of the problem of the Jews. The broader and to him more insistent issue was the vitality of Jewish tradition, spiritual life, and culture—that is, the problem of Judaism. For Ahad Ha'am, the religious-cultural question had to come first. Without a great renascence of Jewish spirit and communal life, neither political activity as such nor the ends it might achieve could be sustained.

As I reflect on how my views about the relation of religion and public life have changed, I find that I have grown more concerned about "the problem of American Judaism" and less worried about "the problem of American Jews." By the latter term I mean the concern to sustain an open society in which Jews suffer no discrimination simply because they are Jews. By the former I mean concern for the kind and quality of Jewish life that Jews in fact lead in the open society.

Most Jewish considerations of the nexus of religion and public life are fixated on the problem of the Jews. Will diversity be compromised or openness diminished by the "intrusion" of religious values into public life? Will Jews become second-class citizens

Alan Mittleman, a rabbi, teaches in the Department of Religion at Muhlenberg College, Allentown, Pennsylvania. He is the author of *Between Kant and Kabbalah: An Introduction to Isaac Breuer's Philosophy of Judaism* (SUNY Press, 1990).

in a more publicly Christian society? These are the typical Jewish questions. But given the unparalleled level of Jewish integration and acceptance in America today, while these questions are not irrelevant, I believe that other questions ought to be asked. What kind of religious life is correlated with the judgment that public affairs ought to be wholly separate from religious values? Is it true, as Jewish spokesmen often argue, that public secularity almost miraculously supports private religious intensity? Or is it the case that public secularity begets, reflexively, the secularization of religious communities that advocate a secularizing strategy? In my view, this is precisely what has happened to Judaism in America.

A strategy of uncompromising secularization directed toward the public realm has become a defining condition of the internal Jewish world. Consequently, a renewal of Jewish life requires a fresh consideration of the connections between religion and public affairs. The renewal of Jewish life and the reappraisal of Jewish social thought are tightly correlated.

How has the problem of Judaism developed? Judaism is not a sectarian or other-worldly religion. While always a religion of the study hall, it is also a religion of marketplaces, courts, and operating rooms. Since the Emancipation, when Jews gave up whatever communal autonomy was left to them in favor of citizenship rights in modern states, these applications of Judaism have withered into academic topics. The applicability of traditional Jewish approaches to public matters remains quite limited even in Israel, although many there are concerned with the recovery of Jewish political and social wisdom. In the diaspora most Jews have compensated for the loss of a public dimension by embracing modern forms of historical action such as Zionism and liberalism.

These concerns point in rather different directions. Zionism is survivalist, liberalism is universalist. The one asserts the primacy of action for the Jewish good. The other appeals to considerations of the common good. Yet both amount phenomenologically to a Jewish public discourse. Both compensate for the loss of a once all-encompassing Jewish world by providing a rationale for action in history and a self-definition of the Jew as an active, political being. Both, in a sense, have become Judaism.

Judaism in America has become a religion of, as Jonathan

Woocher put it, "sacred survival" on the one hand and, I would add, social gospel on the other. Judaism has become the civil religion of an American minority. The periphery has become the center. Values of tolerance, pluralism, fairness, equal rights, and so on have come to be located at the core. Not that these very agreeable values could not have been found to some extent at the core all along; they could have been and were. Rather, there is an artifice and disingenuousness about the process of their thematization. Jewish organizations, for example, antecedently convinced of a woman's right to abortion, have combed Jewish sources for proof-texts and then displayed the results as evidence of Judaism's defense of abortion rights. Indeed, Jewish law supports abortion in some (fairly restricted) cases. That is not the point. What is at issue is the tendentious nature of the exercise.

I take issue here not with where the process winds up but with where it begins. If American Jews had a genuine public philosophy, they would not have to be reduced to adventitious proof-texting. Their consciences would be formed by their subtle and ramified legal tradition. They would argue for the applicability of that tradition to the common good in an appropriately public manner, as the Catholic bishops have tried to do. Instead, they imitate the progressive, yet apodictic pronouncements of Protestant church bodies. Elevated, self-assured moralism substitutes for disciplined argument. And what is said is no different from what might have been said by others. Whatever is distinctive about Judaism has been left out of account, either because it does not accord with the liberal consensus, or because Jews lack a public philosophy of adequate complexity to mediate the values of their tradition to the culture at large. The result is not a lively tension between a distinctive Judaism and the public realm but a redundant repetition by Jews of the culture's (liberal) common sense.

I have argued that the quality and credibility of Judaism is in some sense inseparable from Judaism's engagement with public questions. Because the mode of that engagement heretofore has been dictated by imperatives from the general culture rather than Jewish tradition, Judaism has acquired the cast of a civil religion. Renewal requires that authentic Jewish perspectives be allowed to penetrate our thinking about public matters. As I want to see other groups engage in their own renewal, I welcome their involvement in public discourse. I do not see how authenticity—or simple self-respect—permits anything less.

21

DEBORAH DASH MOORE

PLUS ça change, plus c'est la même chose. Is it possible that the Lubavitchers seeking to erect the Hanukkah menorah in the public square, the Orthodox Jews lobbying for public funding of parochial schools, and the American Jewish Congress writing briefs to remove prayer from the public schools all have a common goal? Don't they all want to make American civil society a bit more comfortable for themselves as Jews? Don't they all desire recognition and respect for Jews from the public authorities?

We seem to have reached the point in the United States where our Jewish religious pluralism generates conflicting visions of the role of religion in the ideal type of civil society. Not only do we no longer agree on what civil society is best for American Jews—we aren't even interested in arguing about the subject among ourselves in order to form a consensus. Instead, having the resources, we pursue our own public agendas. Yet the goal remains the same: to create a civil society in the United States in which Jews are free to be Jews.

This rather modest goal differs substantially from the aims of the groups' various Christian political bedfellows. We do our Jewish opponents an injustice to charge them with seeking to implement the aims of those with whom they cooperate. However much we may deplore the wrong-sightedness of other Jews, we need to

Deborah Dash Moore is director of the American Culture program and professor of religion at Vassar College. She is the editor of the *YIVO Annual*.

recognize that their angle of vision is limited by their position in American Jewish society. To return to my example, Lubavitchers, Orthodox Jews, and American Jewish Congress supporters see the world differently, as Americans and as Jews.

"What ought to be the role of religion in American public life?" this volume asks. It is suggested that religion has been excluded, and we are queried whether it should return. I must admit that I did not notice its absence as successive Supreme Court decisions implemented a greater separation of church and state. Types of religious expressions, their auspices and venues, may have changed since 1945, but to this observer, religion still appears very much present in the public square. Some of this religion is civil, some non-sectarian Christian, some Protestant, and a very small part of it is the voice of the minority religions in the United States. Despite an enlarged understanding of civil society, especially those parts of it directly under governmental auspices, as essentially secular, the United States remains a religious—essentially Christian—nation. If we accept what the polls tell us, substantial majorities of Americans believe and behave according to religious dictates. This widespread and diverse religiosity co-exists comfortably with an increasingly secular civil society. Were I Tocqueville, I might argue that disestablishment produced this flourishing religious voluntarism.

But I am not Tocqueville, and I am supposed to be concerned not just with religion but with Judaism in America. Here my point of view must reflect my position as a Jew and as an American.

I am a Jew who, like most other American Jews, went to public school. Each day I heard the Bible read before I recited the pledge of allegiance. I learned to sing carols and participated in the school's celebration of Christmas. I cannot remember any of the daily Bible readings, but I recall those sections of Tanakh that I studied twice a week under parochial auspices after school. I can remember the Christmas carols, both words and melodies. They made me feel uncomfortable (when I sang them I tried to subvert them)—and I went to school in New York City, surrounded by many other Jewish students and taught by many Jewish teachers. What about those Jews who went to school in Miami? They watched Easter assemblies that re-enacted Christ's death on the cross. How uncomfortable did they feel?

My sons, too, went to public school (still the experience of most American Jews, despite the healthy growth of Jewish day schools). They never heard the Bible read. Instead, they studied Tanakh under parochial auspices after school. They celebrated Christmas but sang seasonal songs without explicitly religious content. They felt less uncomfortable. My niece and nephew in Georgia public schools still sing the religious carols. I suspect they feel as I felt thirty years ago.

Why this long personal account? Because I think that the discussion of religion in American public life too often is conducted in the realm of abstraction with relatively little attention to the lived realities of American Jews. I can understand the Orthodox desire for public monies for parochial schools: they are pursuing their own legitimate self-interest. Similarly, the Lubavitch seek public support of religion because they assume that Jews *should* feel uncomfortable in public schools—they don't belong there. Those of us who think that Jews belong in the public schools and the public square necessarily see things differently. We want to be comfortable in these civil places because they are ours, not just others'. And we assume that government support for Jewish religious symbols, texts, holidays, and songs would make our Christian fellow Americans as uncomfortable as we were when we displayed their symbols, read their texts, and sang their songs. It would be better to develop new sacred symbols, texts, holidays, and songs that we could have in common.

So I guess I have not changed my opinion about religion in public life. I hope that when my grandchildren go to public school they won't have to listen to daily Bible readings or sing religious Christmas songs. I hope they will not see Christmas crèches and trees displayed in front of city hall but rather will view these religious symbols on the grounds of churches and private homes and in their neighbors' living rooms. Nor do I welcome Hanukkah menorahs standing in the public square. I will be satisfied if my grandchildren can admire those in front of synagogues or other Jewish buildings. As for me, I will continue to kindle my own lights and place them in the window for those who care to look, on the assumption that in the religiously plural United States, all public displays of private faith are equally at home.

22

JERRY Z. MULLER

THE capacity of religious groups to offer prudent advice on matters of foreign, military, and economic affairs is rather limited, as experience has shown. Their main significance for our common life lies elsewhere. Our society, though remarkably good at providing freedom and a modicum of prosperity to its citizens, is increasingly inept at conveying to them what freedom is for, that it might have a purpose beyond the endless fulfillment of personal needs and wants. The major role of Judaism in American public life is to act, along with Christianity, to remind men and women of the moral duties and limits that come with an awareness that we are created by God.

Because Judaism is the religion of a small minority, and a religion that regards much of its ritual and symbolic content as binding only upon that minority, Judaism in itself is unlikely to play a major role in shaping the public sphere in America. But much of the ethical content of Judaism that Jews regard as binding upon others is shared with Christianity. Should they therefore seek to advance or to brake the influence of Christianity in American life?

American Jews can view the question of Christianity in public life from three quite different perspectives. The first is that of members of a historically stigmatized sociological minority, con-

Jerry Z. Muller, associate professor of history at the Catholic University of America, is the author of *The Other God that Failed: Hans Freyer and the Deradicalization of German Conservatism* (Princeton, 1987), and the forthcoming *Adam Smith in His Time and Ours: Designing the Decent Society* (The Free Press, 1993).

cerned primarily with minimizing the social, cultural, and economic discrimination or disadvantage. Let us call this *the perspective of minority advancement*. The second is the perspective of a group of people concerned with preserving Judaism as a body of beliefs and symbolic expressions. Let us call this *the perspective of Judaism*. The third is the perspective of citizens concerned with the public good, and especially with preserving social stability and moral decency in the nation. It is concerned with the constitution of the nation, that is, the web of social institutions that provides citizens with manners, standards of character, and reminders of their duties and limits. Let us call this *the perspective of the citizen*.

On issues of religion and public life, the spokesmen for major American Jewish organizations act as if the touchstone of Jewish concern were the Establishment Clause of the First Amendment. They focus not on social institutions that create moral character in the citizenry but on the written Constitution, which they interpret (with disregard both for the intent of its authors and for historical practice) as mandating a "wall between church and state." Approaching the issue mainly from the perspective of minority advancement, they applaud the legally mandated dechristianization of our public life.

Behind the explicit position of organized Jewry on this issue lie the often tacit assumptions that since Christianity is a historic source of anti-Semitism, and since anti-Semitism is bad for the social advancement of Jews, the dechristianization of society ought to be good for Jews. These assumptions are difficult to argue against because they are rarely articulated, but they remain powerful prejudices. Prejudices, of course, are often a sound basis for prudent action because they reflect the lessons of the past. But unexamined prejudices may leave us in thrall to lessons of history that no longer apply because conditions have changed. This particular prejudice is based on more historical experience than some Christians are wont to remember, but on less than some Jews imagine.

It is true that in modern European history, the political ideologies most favorable to the attainment of civic equality for Jews were liberalism and socialism. We tend to forget that for much of the nineteenth century and part of the twentieth, both of these ideologies were militantly secularist, seeking to replace inherited faith with secularism, rationalism, and faith in science. Even Communism, in some periods, was good for Jews, in that it removed some legal and cultural barriers to their social advancement.

To be sure, there were limits to the maxim that equated dechristianization with the increased well-being of Jews. It turned out that the worst enemies of the Jews were the anti-Christians of the radical, racist right and—to a lesser but nevertheless horrifying extent—the radical left. Nevertheless, from approximately the 1940s through the 1970s, the remarkable social and economic success of American Jews was accompanied and in part made possible by a decline in anti-Semitism; and these years of growing cultural and material comfort saw the extrusion of Christianity from parts of the public realm, partially through the actions of the courts enforcing new-found interpretations of the Establishment Clause. Jews inclined by their European past to believe that a dechristianized public realm worked to their benefit could find their European assumptions buttressed by American experience. To the extent that Jewish interests are defined in terms of minority advancement, the dechristianization of America remains good for the Jews.

But does this perpective adequately define Jewish interests in America? What if Jews view themselves as part of a people constituted by their covenant with God? What if they view themselves as citizens concerned with the social and moral well-being of the republic?

I believe that the contemporary extrusion of religion—and above all, of the nominal religion of the majority—from more and more areas of collective life has been harmful to the American constitution (that is, the network of character-building institutions), and hence ought to be a source of concern for Jews in their capacity as enlightened citizens. This proposition has been argued by Irving Kristol for years, and I have found that it makes the most sense of the cultural phenomena around us, as both the mass culture and the elite culture become ever more debased. But one cannot conclude, alas, that *wie es sich kristolt, so judelt es sich*: most American Jews remain not so much unconvinced by Kristol's argument as oblivious to it. My own views on this matter have altered, in part as my knowledge of American history has grown, in part because the nature of liberalism has changed, and in part because the changing role of the state in advanced industrial societies makes the application of "strict separation" doctrines more deleterious than it would have been in the past.

The part that various forms of Christianity have played in American history as a civilizing agent is rarely appreciated by Jews (or by Christians, for that matter, who are largely protected from such knowledge in the public schools). I refer, not to the role of the churches in the great political crusades such as abolition and civil rights, but to the less dramatic yet no less important promotion of more mundane virtues. By providing the structures of belief and the social institutions that reinforced "respectable" behavior, Christianity time and again created a modicum of decency among men and women who would otherwise have been wild, as in the "wild West," an apt description of many regions in this nation's history that were on the frontier either geographically or socially. Within living memory, Christians were organized for the support of "decency," i.e., a public realm and mass culture in which the inhabitants (Christian and Jewish and otherwise) could raise their children without the constant danger of exposing them to the most debased views of how men and women ought to relate to one another.

What is bought and sold in the marketplace of a capitalist democracy depends upon the balance of cultural forces. Unless countervailing pressures are provided either by the state or by the cultural institutions of civil society, cultural commodities will tend to appeal to the lowest in man. As the influence of the most historically significant cultural institutions in civil society—the Christian churches—has eroded, we have been left with an increasingly degraded cultural reality. It takes its greatest psychological and spiritual toll on those outside the structures of family and church, but in one way or another it takes its toll on all of us.

Once I believed that the strict separation of religion and state served the public interest, since religious influences would continue to be felt through cultural, educational, and social institutions outside the sphere of government. I have come to reconsider that view, because it fails to take account of the changing relationship between government and civil society in America. For reasons that are probably inevitable, as society becomes more mobile, the role of government in cultural, educational, and social institutions tends to expand. Most educational and charitable activity now goes on in governmental institutions, such as public schools, that are prohibited from conveying any religious understanding of moral demands—indeed any moral demands at all—lest they offend some moral minority. Thus the major character-building agencies of our society are rendered increasingly incapable of teaching that some desires are more morally worthy of fulfillment than others, or that life has some higher purpose than the gratification of desires.

The practice of public education has thus come to match the ethos of contemporary liberalism. Liberalism once meant opposing excessive government interference in the realm of personal decisions. Such an understanding had as its necessary corollary a stress on the importance of non-governmental social and cultural institutions in conveying and enforcing standards of moral behavior. Contemporary liberalism, by contrast, often opposes the "interference" of any social or cultural institution in personal behavior. This perverse understanding of liberty makes contemporary liberalism largely incapable of offering resistance to the degrading of the common culture to what is lowest in man. Since human nature abhors a vacuum, the moral space abandoned by the best and the brightest is filled by commercialized appeals to the worst and the dumbest.

Such problems can have no easy resolution. In view of the historic role of religious groups in maintaining the social institutions that foster moral decency, and in view of the increasing inability of governmentally controlled institutions to fulfill basic character-building functions, one plausible innovation lies in expanding educational and charitable institutions run by non-governmental associations, including religious institutions. Public policy might aim at reinvigorating the character-building institutions of civil society—for example, by providing tax dollars or tax deductions for tuition at religiously based schools. Such policies would require that we abandon the currently dominant interpretation of the Establishment Clause of the First Amendment and restore the historic meaning of that amendment, which prevented the state from legally establishing—that is, favoring with official state support—a particular denomination.

From the perspective of minority advancement, would an America in which Christians were more consciously Christian be bad for the Jews? Would it increase social or cultural discrimination against them? To answer with certainty is impossible. But in the decades since the Holocaust (indeed, in part because of the Holocaust) the major Christian denominations have come to terms with the historical legitimacy of Judaism to a degree once unimaginable and still largely unappreciated by most American Jews. If, in fact, Jews were more conspicuously "other" in a more Christian America, that otherness would be in keeping with Jewish religious self-understanding. To know oneself as Jewish and in a condition of *galut* is to regard oneself as other: the fear of seeming other varies directly with the degree of estrangement from Judaism.

This brings us to the perspective of Jews as adherents of Judaism in America. From this perspective, too, Jews have a great deal to lose from the continuation of the status quo, and a good deal to gain from a redrawing of the map of religion and public life. The conservation of Judaism in America is an uphill struggle. Recent survey data on rates of intermarriage ought to remind us that in the only historical example of continuous Jewish existence in a liberal society—that of England—Jews tended to disappear as Jews by the fifth generation. Insofar as Jewishness is reduced to a matter of ethnicity and of historical accident, it will become an increasingly marginal factor in the major life decisions of Americans of Jewish origin. In a society as open as that of the United States, and in a population as educated as American Jewry, Jews are fated for complete absorption into non-Jewish culture unless they are intellectually prepared to confront that culture on Jewish grounds.

Such preparation is very difficult without day-school education. American Jewry will in the future be smaller in numbers, perhaps much smaller. Whether the remnant will be a saving remnant depends largely on the strength of Jewish day-school education, which will in turn depend in part on the availability of government funding to cover part of the costs of such schools. Ironically, even some of those active in improving the quality of Jewish education diminish its impact by their abhorrence of religion in the public sphere. By trivializing the role of religion in public life, they diminish its role in personal life as well, so that Jewish education becomes a matter of "parochial" interest in the negative sense.

Perhaps, therefore, American Jews ought to reconsider their prejudices about the role of religion in the public sphere. To the extent that they are citizens concerned for the common welfare, and to the extent that they are Jews concerned about the fate of Judaism and of Jewish values in the larger society, they must view the issue through something other than the lenses of a once-stigmatized minority concerned primarily with removing any conceivable barriers to individual advancement.

23

DAVID NOVAK

C ERTAINLY since the first World War, with the rise to promi-
nence of the major secular Jewish organizations in America,
the official line of the American Jewish "Establishment" has been
that the strictest possible separation of religion and the state is
something that is good for Jews and good for America. The clear
implication is that the more secular American society is, the better.

I would argue that this line has not been good either for Jews or
for America.

It has not been good for Jews because it has relegated Judaism
(along with Christianity) to the realm of the private. Now despite
the great value Americans place on privacy, they do so by public
means. Those who speak of a "right to privacy" do so in the context
of a constitutional (that is, a public) guarantee. It is the self-
limitation of the public realm that makes room for the private.

If the public realm is where the important moral issues are
decided (important being defined as receiving more effort and
attention), and if Judaism is something private, Judaism then seems
to become something of secondary moral import at best. However,
Judaism does not survive very well, let alone thrive, in an atmosphere where it is not the primary moral authority in the lives
of Jews. According to classical Jewish teaching, the whole world

David Novak is Edgar M. Bronfman Professor of Modern Judaic Studies
at the University of Virginia. He is founder and vice president of the
Union for Traditional Judaism. His most recent book is *Jewish Social Ethics*
(Oxford University Press, 1992).

was created for the sake of the Torah; the Torah cannot simply be a subordinate part of a larger whole.

This does not mean that Jews can live with moral integrity only in a society Judaically constituted (a society that does not at present exist, even in the State of Israel). Judaism surely teaches Jews to respect the authority of any society that is founded on right, not might, and that allows Jews to practice the commandments of the Torah. Nevertheless, this public moral requirement is only Jewish if explicitly constituted Judaically. Jews cannot simply be "Jews inside and human beings outside," as a nineteenth-century poet, over-enamored with the Enlightenment, put the matter. In retrospect, that slogan turned out to be a prescription for assimilation.

Current Jewish experience has confirmed the truth of traditional Judaic teaching. The remarkable resurgence of religious commitment among some American Jews—often the best and the brightest (coupled, alas, with the increasing indifference and assimilation of others)—can be traced to a stance that runs directly against the relegation of Judaism to the realm of the private.

The best example of this religious resurgence is the Jewish day-school movement, which is now endorsed by every segment of religious Jewry. Schools are public institutions; even if they do not receive public funds (a point many supporters of religious schools, Jews and others, argue need not be the case on constitutional grounds), they do receive public accreditation and other types of official recognition. There is now a clear consensus that this type of education provides a far better source of Jewish identity for Jewish children in America than education that can only supplement the education offered in the public (that is, state) schools. To cite just one positive result, a considerable segment of the younger leadership of the American Jewish community is made up of graduates of these Jewish day schools.

This encouraging situation is not attributable to the efforts of the strict separationists. Rather, it is the product of those Jews who would like to see more, not less, public support for these schools and for religion in general. Most of the strict separationists seem to have been primarily concerned with the support of secularism in American life. The greatest expenditures of their time and money seem to have been for lawsuits and other forms of public protest against what they see as the encroachment of religion into American public life.

As for American democracy itself, the strict separation of religion from public life has not been good, either. (By "religion" I actually mean "religions"—that is, religious pluralism. Clearly no responsible Jew could be a supporter of an official state religion or anything like "Christian America.") Strict separation has not been good for American democracy, because the nation's true roots are religious and not secular. The relationship with God is the primary human right and duty from which all other rights and duties flow. (The recognition that this relationship presupposes political liberty in order to be freely affirmed—hence properly affirmed—guarantees the rights of those non-believers who choose not to exercise the right and fulfill the duty.) Without this foundation, American democracy can be based only on a type of secularism that cannot allow, let alone guarantee, the place of religions in the public realm. That is something that neither Jews nor Christians can accept with moral integrity.

Strict separationism is bad both for Jews and for America for essentially the same reason. I believe that Jews are meant to be much more than just another ethnic group, concerned only with our own particularism. Judaism teaches that Jews are to be God's witnesses to the whole world (Isaiah 43:9–10). That witness can be made only in an atmosphere where Jews can live according to the singular requirements involved in our covenant with God. This presupposes an environment in which the human relationship with God, in all its plurality, is publicly respected and is thus publicly influential. What is good for Jews is, in this sense at least, good for the world. Strict separationism, because of its secularist foundation, is inconsistent with what American Jews ought to desire for themselves and for the society in which they live.

24

CYNTHIA OZICK

FIRST, a comment on my eligibility for this discussion. I am primarily a writer of fiction, and when on occasion I have ventured into the essay, it has usually been with a pointedly literary purpose. I have no qualifications—or capacity—for discourse on public issues. What I come equipped with, then, is not a set of arguments but something quite other: my childhood dread of a school-imposed Christmas, and my undiluted memory of the shock of public punishment for refusing to sing Christian hymns at school assembly. The pain of this inescapably overt and helpless nonconformism, forced on a diffident and profoundly frightened Jewish child, has left its lifelong mark.

That is why—this suffering recollection of having been put on display on a platform as a recalcitrant enemy of the polity—I remain unreconstructed on the subject of the unadorned public square and what is, in my view, the still entirely viable heritage of separation. You may exclaim: "What stupid teachers you had! How insensitive to treat a child like that! If only you'd had kind or intelligent teachers, how much more yielding you'd be on this matter." But the kindness or intelligence of teachers is hardly the issue. Stupidity will always be in good supply. What we ought to work for is an absence of opportunity for stupidity to take action. The wall of separation protects against just such opportunity.

Religion, it seems to me, is surely weak and moribund if it must

Cynthia Ozick is a novelist and essayist. Her most recent collection of essays is *Metaphor & Memory* (Vintage).

rely on public space to make its claims and assert its influence. Of course it is harder, speaking historically, for Christianity (and for Islam) to relinquish the public square than it is for Judaism, because "relinquishment" is indeed what American separationism requires of Christianity. In almost every nation but our own, Christianity has not been accustomed to go without at least nominal recognition or fealty by the state. Judaism, by contrast, under both Christianity and Islam, has felt the force of that "under," and has not experienced any connection with sovereign status for two thousand years; hence there is no authority or public influence to be surrendered. Christian restraint, then, must be learned, while Jewish restraint in this respect comes, as we say, with the territory. (Except when the territory is Israel since its resuscitation in 1948; but Israel—like Britain, Sweden, and Holland, and unlike the United States—is not an Enlightenment construction.)

It is lately being proposed by some Jewish thinkers that the alternative to a religious presence in public places is a tendency toward paganism, vandalism, a diminution of public morality, the annihilation of ordinary expectations of decent conduct in the streets. "Separation favors paganism," Milton Himmelfarb declares. He means by this that irreligion fosters barbarism—a conclusion it would be dangerous to disagree with. The famous flower children ended up as Charles Manson. "Doing one's thing" produced Milwaukee's Dahmer. "Make love not war" brought on public licentiousness on a hugely tragic scale; promiscuity's diseases will have killed more young men and women than died in Korea and Vietnam together. But to say that irreligion encourages savagery is not the same as asserting that separationism favors paganism. Separationism need not result in irreligion. There is, between irreligious barbarism and secularist separationism, a *tertium quid*.

For this I return to my childhood. I was still in grammar school when the "released time" program was instituted—an undertaking that used hours of the public-school day to send pupils out to local churches for religious instruction. As the only Jew in my class, I had no place to go, precisely because I *had* a place to go; but my religious instruction began after school hours, in the daily *heder*, and did not take time away from Norse myths or arithmetic and vocabulary tests. Consequently, while the others were away I sat in the classroom drawing pictures, alone with an imprisoned teacher: pointless prisoners together.

People like to say that the *heder* was an educational failure, and to an extent that is true. Its teaching was inefficient and often ineffective; it did not, by and large, produce scholars of Judaism. But the charge of wholesale failure misrepresents. No one who went diligently to *heder* after school was left unprovided for by its perspectives and its premises, however shallowly they may have been conveyed.

What the *heder* taught was this: that there is an urgent connection between study and ethical conduct, between the Hebrew alphabet that is the entrance to the Commandments and simple *menschlikh-kayt*. And one learned this just by showing up, even if nothing more than *alef-beys* sank in, even if one sat the whole time looking longingly out the window into the street, where other kids were cavorting freely at stickball or potsy. The *heder* itself—just *going* to it—was a primary discipline, a barrier against wildness, looseness, recklessness, remoteness, isolation, alienation, neutered secularism. My afternoons in a poor little room with a young Rabbi Chaim Meskin (who afterward went on to more distinguished things) supplied more than the alphabet and the opening of Genesis; what was given, and what was received (even by the most restless), was the idea of civilization. There was a clear difference between the Jewish child who went to *heder* and the Jewish child who was merely sent to "Sunday school" for an hour once a week (and a still greater chasm between these and the unfortunate child of parents who put a measured quantity of "fresh air" above any measure of religious literacy). The difference was not so much in information or knowledge as in moral seriousness. *Heder* kids understood—understood for life—that, no matter how much mischief they made right under the rabbi's nose, no matter how much they slouched across their desks after a five-hour day in "regular" school, what they were learning was uprightness. What they were learning was responsibility.

With regard to religion in public places, responsibility is the point. The *heder* was supported by the congregational community, which paid the rabbi/teacher. There was a school fee besides, but those who could not afford it were quietly admitted anyhow; in my class, which included foster children, no one knew whose parents paid and whose did not. What counted was the *heder* itself. Its value for Jewish children, and for the society the children would grow up to join, was *felt*—above all other values. The *heder* of its own free will did not usurp time from the public school or money from the public treasury, and certainly it did not demand that its celebrations, its liturgy, and its symbols announce themselves from the rooftops. The *heder* did not consider itself in a state of spiritual poverty or deprivation because it remained officially unrecognized in the public square. Its mission was to send out into the world serious human beings who would be incapable of defiling or degrading the public order. The *heder*, in taking on responsibility for itself, took on public responsibility as well.

So the choice, it seems to me, is not in the least between separationism and irreligion. What our faith communities would be wise to choose is religious responsibility undertaken autonomously, independently, and on cherished private ground, turning their backs on anyone, however estimable or prudential, who proposes that the church steeple ought to begin to lean on the town hall roof. Church steeples, like the people who worship beneath them, are more effective when upright.

The solution to the advance of public paganism is not the deterioration or destruction of the wall of separation. What this country needs is a whole lot of *heders*, in one form or another, and of every persuasion.

25

JAKOB J. PETUCHOWSKI

THE writer of this article does *not* believe in the Trinity. He does not believe that Jesus of Nazareth was either a part of the Godhead or the Messiah expected by the Jews. In other words, he is not a Christian.

But the writer of these lines also dissociates himself completely from the battle waged each winter by various Jewish organizations against the festival of Christmas, or at least against the public observance of Christmas. For one thing, although he does not celebrate Christmas in his own home, he rather likes the sights, the sounds, and the smells of Christmas. Nor is he beyond relishing such traditional German Christmas delicacies as *Lebkuchen* and *Stollen*—coming, as he does, from a German-Jewish background where those bakery goods figured prominently in the observance of the Jewish winter festival of Hanukkah. Colorfully decorated Christmas trees and crèches, in the homes of Christian friends and in public places, delight his eyes; the sound of Christmas carols is music to his ears; and he avidly follows the pageantry of the Papal Midnight Mass on his TV screen.

Still, all that is a matter of mere externals. What really intrigues him is the fact that millions of his non-Jewish fellow human beings

Jakob J. Petuchowski, who died in 1992, was the Sol and Arlene Bronstein Professor of Judaeo-Christian Studies and the Research Professor of Jewish Theology and Liturgy at Hebrew Union College in Cincinnati; the Albert Plotkin Professor of Judaic Studies at Arizona State University in Tempe; and the part-time rabbi of Temple B'nai Israel, Laredo, Texas. This essay previously appeared in *First Things*.

are celebrating the birthday of a *Jewish* child. And they are doing so by extolling the values of peace and good will. All the more misplaced, he thinks, are the efforts by some supposedly Jewish organizations to arouse, through their battles against Christmas symbols in public places, the ill will and resentment of Christians—at the very time when, more than at other times of the year, the Christian religion inspires its followers with irenic and philanthropic sentiments.

Suppose that half of the world, including the United States, were to take note of the contributions made to human thought by Baruch Spinoza, the seventeenth-century thinker of Jewish origin, by instituting an annual celebration of his birthday—including the public display of Spinoza's lens-grinding workshop. Would the Jewish organizations now fighting public Christmas displays also fight the public observance of Spinoza's birthday? Hardly. In fact, they might even welcome it—even though Spinoza severely criticized the faith of his Jewish ancestors and was excommunicated by the rabbinical authorities of Amsterdam.

Or what would happen if there were an annual International Sigmund Freud Day, including public displays of replicas of the couch that once stood in Freud's Vienna consulting room? Would Jewish organizations now fighting public Christmas displays fight that display, too? Hardly. They might even welcome it—even though Freud proudly proclaimed his own atheism, and included the religion of his Jewish ancestors among the world's religions, all of which he described as illusions.

What, then, is so different about celebrating the birthday of that Palestinian Jew through whose influence, as already noted by the great twelfth-century Jewish thinker Moses Maimonides, the words of Israel's Torah have been spread to the far corners of the earth? Why does the public celebration of the birthday of Jesus of Nazareth, including the public display of replicas of the Bethlehem crèche, arouse such animosity?

The reasons are varied and complex. Tradionally, despite its role in spreading major Jewish teachings throughout the world, Christianity has not been, to put it mildly, an unmixed blessing for Jews. Not only the words of the Torah were spread throughout the world in Jesus' name; that same name was also invoked when, throughout the centuries, Christians murdered Jews by the thousands, burned them alive, confiscated their goods, restricted the way in which they could earn their livelihoods, and confined them to overcrowded and unsanitary quarters. The Christian ideals of peace and good will did not extend beyond the entrance of the ghetto. This may no longer be the case today. But Jews have long memories. To many of them, the sign of the Cross is still a reminder of pogroms and persecutions. Their attitude toward Christianity and toward Christianity's founder is, therefore, highly ambivalent.

That is particularly true of those Jews—and they tend to be the most Orthodox followers of the faith—whose own personal and family background in Eastern Europe approximated most closely the conditions of Jewish life in the Christian Middle Ages. Those Jews certainly cannot be expected to "enjoy" Christmas.

Yet, and here we come to an apparent paradox, these East European Orthodox Jews are *not* in the forefront of those who protest most vociferously against the public display of Christmas symbols—in fact, most of them have nothing at all to do with the organizations that lead this battle in the name of *the* "Jewish Community."

That battle is led by a different type of Jew altogether. He or she is most likely to be a secularist of Jewish origin, who has no use for any kind of religion, including the religion into which he or she was born. And in that battle, the secularist of Jewish origin is likely to be joined by a fellow Jew of the Reform Jewish denomination, which, in its increasingly radical departures from tradional Jewish belief and practice, is more and more becoming a wing of American secularism. Such Jews seek alliances with all the other secularist forces in the country that want to denude the "public square" of every last trace of religious influence. They keep insisting upon a strict enforcement of the separation of church and state—enforcement to a degree certainly not anticipated by the founders of the republic.

In other words, what we are really dealing with in this annual battle against public Christian observance is not so much a "Jewish" attack as a *secularist* one—with some of the prominent secularists identifying themselves as Jews. They are the same people who fight non-denominational prayers in public schools, the use of public-school facilities for meetings of high-school religious-interest groups, and state support of private schools. They fight with equal vigor the attempts by other Jewish groups to have Jewish religious symbols exhibited alongside the Christian ones, such as the efforts of the Chabad-Lubavitch group of Orthodox Jews to place a Hanukkah candelabrum on the public square when a Christmas tree is put up there (which would be a fitting demonstration of America's religious pluralism). They are, in other words, not singling out Christianity. They are against the public manifestation of religion *per se*—even (or perhaps particularly) the religion of their own ancestors.

Using the First Amendment as authority for the campaign against the public display of any and all religious symbols seems to involve the demand that the state "establish" Secularism as the official religion of the United States—a rather curious use of the First Amendment, to say the least. But even if one were to grant, for argument's sake, that the lawyers employed by the American Jewish Congress, the (Reform) Union of American Hebrew Congregations, and similar organizations have established the "true" meaning of the First Amendment, i.e., that it really and truly rules out the public display of a crèche or a Hanukkah candelabrum, one would still be entitled to wonder what those organizations hope to gain by stirring up animosities every winter.

Traditional Jewish teaching includes the principle of *liphnim mishurat hadin* (cf. Babylonian Talmud *Baba Qamma* 100a and elsewhere), which means that, on occasion, it is preferable not to make use of the full extent to which the law, strictly interpreted, entitles one to go. For there is, after all, a "higher law," adumbrated in Deuteronomy 12:28, "You shall do what is good and right in the sight of the Lord your God." Several passages in Jesus' Sermon on the Mount seem to incorporate that principle. It is not a case of "abolishing" the law but rather, if one so desires—and if one does so to one's own, and not the other person's, hurt—of not pressing the law to its fullest extent. This restraint, though it may not be an everyday occurrence in traditional Jewish life, manifests a higher degree of piety. Some of the ancient rabbis even sought to find a biblical basis for such transcendence of biblical law.

It seems to this writer that, even if the strict constructionists of the separation of church and state could demonstrate beyond a shadow of a doubt that the public display of Christmas symbols infringes upon that "separation," Jews might still prefer to abide by the principle of *liphnim mishurat hadin*, of not running to the courts in order to get the law to interfere with the spontaneous expression of their neighbors' piety. After all, what are we to think of a "Judaism" so weak that it feels threatened by the display of a crèche at City Hall, or by the sound of a Christmas carol at a public-school assembly? Why not, then, show some generosity at a season when Christians celebrate the birth of the Jew in whose name they proclaim peace and good will to humankind?

To be quite honest, it is not only a matter of generosity. Life in the medieval Christian world—in which, by the way, we no longer live—certainly was no bed of roses for the Jews. But Jews fared infinitely *worse* in those modern societies from which the God of Abraham and of Jesus had been banished. If Jews cannot forget the Middle Ages, they owe it to themselves to remember the most recent past, too. One could argue, therefore, that the very self-interest of the Jews is at stake in preventing the United States from becoming a totally godless society.

Jews cannot accept the dogmas and the theology associated with the Christmas story; they would cease to be Jews if they did. Nor would they be acting in good faith if, without accepting the Christian belief structure, they were to celebrate Christmas in their own homes. (And it does not help much if they try to justify the Christmas tree in their homes by saying that it was originally a pagan, rather than a Christian, custom—as if Judaism approved of paganism!) But they can still recognize in the *Christian* observance of Christmas one of the factors that help maintain the religious character of our society—in which Jews, with their own beliefs and practices and with their very lives, have a considerable stake.

That is why this writer will continue to wish his Christian friends a "Merry Christmas" at Yuletide, and rejoice in the fact that those friends join the angelic choir in proclaiming glory to God in the highest and peace among humankind on earth. He will most certainly not object at all to the public display of his friends' symbols of religious faith. Indeed, he will continue to be moved by awe and wonder that, through the influence of one of his own remote cousins, some of the words of Judaism's Torah have been spread to the far corners of the earth.

26

DENNIS PRAGER

SECULAR Jewish activists have been doing both America and American Jewry great harm in their unrelenting war against any manifestation of religion outside the church or synagogue and the home.

The harm to Jews has been the raising of a generation of "Jews for Nothing." Many American Jews resent—correctly, I believe— "Jews for Jesus." Yet Jewish fears of "Jews for Jesus" have been utterly disproportionate to the threat. The few "Jews for Jesus" are a negligible threat to Jewish welfare and survival, while Jews for Nothing pose an almost fatal threat to American Jewry.

The harm to American society at large is that we have also been raising non-Jews with no commitments to anything higher than themselves. And when these products of our secular world do have commitments, they are increasingly to trees and to sea otters rather than to human beings, and certainly not to anything so quaint as God, character development, or the holy.

In lectures to American Jews, one of the points I emphasize is the tragic irony that the Jews, the people who brought God into the world, are today among the leaders of virtually every American movement dedicated to removing God and religion from the world. To cite one of too many possible examples, the aggressively secularist American Jewish Congress welcomed the Supreme Court ruling

Dennis Prager is co-author of *The Nine Questions People Ask About Judaism* and of *Why the Jews? The Reason for Antisemitism*. He is the editor of *Ultimate Issues*, hosts a nightly radio program (KABC Los Angeles), and is president of the Micah Center for Ethical Monotheism.

upholding a state ban on the posting of the Ten Commandments in public high schools. We Jews gave the world the Ten Commandments, and the secular Jews of the American Jewish Congress and the non-Jewish Jews of the ACLU devote their lives to taking them back.

How this happened is a theme that Rabbi Joseph Telushkin and I developed in the chapter on non-Jewish Jews in our book *Why the Jews? The Reason for Antisemitism*. Suffice it to say here that activist secular Jews *are* highly religious, and they do profoundly believe in shaping society according to their beliefs. The problem is that their religion is not Judaism. It is liberalism.

Liberalism possesses every characteristic of a religion, with the exception of God-based ethics. Liberalism is a leap of faith (to, for example, the inherent goodness of man); it offers idealistic passion and a community of fellow true believers (in the myriad liberal organizations). It offers commitments to things higher than self; it even has saints (liberal heroes and liberal organizations such as the ACLU) and of course villains (conservatives, particularly neo-conservatives, Ronald Reagan). It has its own sacred scriptures (e.g., the Constitution as they understand it), its inviolable laws (just as Orthodox Jews venerate and rely on Halakah, liberal Jews venerate and rely on American law), and even a devil who causes all evil (socioeconomic forces).

Thus, before addressing the question of how religion should enter into public life, it is imperative that we recognize two things:

First, secular religion, i.e., liberalism, has no problem whatsoever with imposing its agenda on American life. If liberalism could be officially listed as a religion, we could then use the Establishment Clause against liberal authoritarianism just as liberals use it against religious authoritarianism.

Second, were it not for the Judeo-Christian tradition (I am quite aware of the many differences between Judaism and Christianity, but I am equally well aware of the values that the two religions share), America would have been a moral and economic wasteland. And that is precisely what America will become without religion.

Having said this, I do wish to emphasize the importance of separating church and state. The mixture of the two has never been good, not historically in Christendom, and not today in Israel. It is also particularly bad for religion, which becomes weak and corrupt when it can rely on the state for its force.

The dilemma is then quite clear: Without religious values, America will rapidly crumble; yet the state and religion must be kept separate. How can we reconcile these divergent realities?

The answer lies in one of the least common traits in contemporary American life—moderation. The secular government must hold *as an American value* that cultivating religion is a good thing for purely practical reasons. Even an atheist can acknowledge the negative ramifications of the death of God in society—e.g., the late Michael Harrington in his book *The Politics of God's Funeral*.

That is why this Jew has no problem with a crèche at City Hall. Only secular extremists can find offense in such an innocuous governmental display of religion. (But have you noticed that there is no such thing in the American lexicon as secular extremists, only religious extremists?)

Not only does this Jew not object to a crèche in City Hall: I think it can actually benefit Jews. I want Jewish children to ask their parents questions about who they are. Quite aside from my belief that a vibrant Christianity is indispensable to American life, I want Christianity to be vibrant in America for selfish Jewish reasons. When the non-Jews are religious, the Jews stay Jewish; and when the majority culture believes in nothing, most Jews will believe in nothing.

Thus, I want Christians to fight the battle against abortion on demand even though, as a Jew, I strongly disagree about abortion being murder. For the secular liberal view of the fetus as of no more value than a decayed tooth—what else can "a woman can do what she wants with her own body" mean?—is frightening. Moreover, that Jewish organizations should hold such a position constitutes one of the gravest Jewish sins, a *khillul Hashem* (desecration of God's name).

I want the Ten Commandments taught, not just displayed, in public schools. I do not want young people to get a secular brainwash, going from kindergarten through college without once having been challenged to look at life through religious eyes.

Most of all, I want religious men and women to advocate religion in the public square (not through government). But I mean religion, not liberalism and not conservatism. When the National Conference of Catholic Bishops sounds identical to Jesse Jackson and the secular left on the role of American force in a world of evil, I wonder whether this is Catholicism or liberalism that I am hearing. When Protestants start flirting with or even embracing pacifism, a doctrine that holds that it is morally preferable to allow Dr. Mengele to continue to perform medical experiments on men, women, and children rather than to kill him, I see why many people regard liberal Protestantism as secularism with Christ's name added on.

My ideal is a secular government and a religious society. But with every passing day I see America moving further and further from this ideal, becoming militantly, nihilistically secular. Only if Jews and Christians begin pointing out that it is not socioeconomic conditions but the decline of religion that is the greatest single cause of the moral decline of our country do we have a prayer. Unless we do so, prayer won't help.

27

EARL RAAB

Two American Jewish concerns about the role of religion in society, both appropriate, often seem in conflict. One is the desire for a milieu that will allow Jews and their practice of Judaism to flourish without impediment. In pursuit of that goal, Jews have often invoked the First Amendment prescription about church-state separation.

The second concern has to do with the condition of social morality. When Thomas Jefferson wrote that "the practice of morality [is] necessary for the well-being of society," he meant by morality those fundamental standards of decency among human beings that the major religions commonly affirm. Those standards generally correspond to the universal Noachian commandments about the sanctity of life, person, family, and procedures for justice.

Moral standards like these are indeed essential to the kind of society to which all people are entitled, and which Jews and Judaism *require*, in order to survive physically and to flourish and contribute spiritually. And such standards are inseparable from religion.

Rabbi Johanan wrote that "if the Torah had not been given, we could have learned modesty from the cat, [aversion to] robbery from the ant, chastity from the dove, and good manners from the cock." Perhaps. But those are not the characteristics we are most likely to learn from the animals. Neither an intellectual grasp of

Earl Raab is director of the Nathan Perlmutter Institute for Jewish Advocacy at Brandeis University and director emeritus of the Jewish Community Relations Council of the San Francisco area.

"natural law" nor pragmatic ethics has provided societies with a durable base of social morality.

But Jefferson added this comment: "The interests of society require observation of those moral principles only in which all religions agree. . . ."

Those organized religions that alone can provide and refresh a common moral base do not customarily agree on the consequent social and political policies. Isaiah enjoined us to turn swords into plowshares, while Joel urged that we turn plowshares into swords. Many churches in the ante-bellum South supported the slavery that many churches in the North excoriated. Some religious groups believe that the sanctity of life is debased, others that it is enhanced, by capital punishment—or by abortion rights. And so on, and on.

These disparate secular, doctrinal, or circumstantial judgments by disparate religious groups do not demean the common moral base. A respect for religious culture must be balanced with restraints against allowing the secular, doctrinal, or circumstantial judgments of any particular religious groups to dominate the political process.

The Establishment and Free Exercise clauses of the First Amendment are in constant tension. My perception of what is required to hold them in balance has changed over the past forty years. I do not worry as much now about the "foot-in-the-door" syndrome. Most Jewish organizations still oppose the idea of silent prayer in the schools, not because they consider silent prayer dangerous or unconstitutional in itself, but because they think it is the foot in the door behind which the body of open and sectarian prayer can materialize.

But in the last forty years, the vitality of the mainstream religious culture has been eroding, while resistance to sectarian dominance has not. There is no imminent danger that sectarian religious prayer will become legally prevalent in the public schools. And, if sectarian prayer is not a serious danger, then the exclusion of silent prayer is not only a signal against the religious culture but also an unwarranted interference with the free exercise of religion.

By the same token, the multiple or non-sectarian expression of religious sentiment at high-school graduation ceremonies does not concern me as it once did. Permitting the multiple expression of religion in public places may be more desirable at this time than prohibiting such expression.

Judge Learned Hand said that the canons of the First Amendment "are not jural concepts at all in the ordinary sense; and in application they turn out to be no more than admonitions of moderation." And the fulcrum of moderation, like that of balance, shifts as circumstances change.

None of this means that Jews should relax their wariness against official practices that subordinate either Jews or Judaism. Nor should the disingenuous argument prevail that if a practice is permissible it is therefore commendable. I do not believe that government vouchers for attendance at religious schools would violate the constitutional balance between separation and free exercise, any more than does tax exemption for churches and synagogues. But I would still oppose most voucher systems for private schools as contrary to the public interest (and the Jewish interest) on other than church-state grounds.

There is also the danger that in arguing for more headroom for a "religious culture," we could come to expect too much from that culture. A religion-plated society is not a religious society. One Christian clergy group opposed any Christmas celebrations in the schools on the grounds that they would be inevitably reductionist.

Nevertheless, a society that is antagonistic or even rigorously neutral to the body of traditional religions will not serve the Jews well. It is easy to lock in an automatic position against any religion-friendly act by the state. It is more difficult constantly to seek a balance between two requirements for America and American Jews (to extend Jefferson's terms beyond his own meaning): a society whose demeanor will nurture those traditional religions that provide the moral base "necessary for the well-being of [that] society," and a society whose moral base will reflect "those moral principles only in which all [those] religions agree."

28

SAMUEL RABINOVE

W HAT ought to be the role of religions (plural) in American public life? My own "standing on one foot" answer would be this: an active, vibrant, constructive role on behalf of humane values. In our pluralistic society, of course, different religions and religious leaders may hold divergent views as to the proper content of humane values.

Without question, religious and spiritual values have contributed immeasurably to human progress from barbarism to what we now call civilization. I say this notwithstanding my painful awareness of the centuries-old nightmares of religious bigotry and cruelty throughout the world—a dismal history that some religionists, perhaps understandably, would rather forget. As we well know, we need not go back to antiquity to retrieve this record—it has happened all too often in this century, and in many parts of the world it is happening right now. For centuries, most religions condoned the monstrous evil of slavery. They limited severely the role of women in society as well as within their faith and practiced a sexism that persists today in many religious quarters. Until recently, many Christian churches actively taught contempt for the Jews. Virtually all religions, alas, have much of which to repent. Yet the best of religious thought and values is critically needed in America today.

Samuel Rabinove is legal director of the American Jewish Committee. He has taught at Hebrew Union College in Los Angeles and is a member of the Religious Liberty Committee of the National Council of Churches.

Nothing in the U.S. Constitution says that religions cannot play a vital role in American public life, and they certainly should play such a role. Separation of church and state does not mean separation of church and society. But clergy should not forget that the Constitution makes no mention of Jesus, or Moses, or even of God. Does this mean that the framers were hostile to Christian or Jewish religion? Not at all. But they were surely hostile to any fusion of religion and government. They knew in their bones that this country had been settled mainly by Christians—Puritans, Quakers, Baptists, Lutherans, Catholics, Huguenots, Mennonites, and many others—who were fleeing oppression in Europe at the hands of other Christians who controlled the machinery of government, and who believed they were doing the Lord's will when they savagely persecuted dissident minority sects, both Christian and Jewish. The framers knew, too, that religious oppression had already happened here: for example, under the Puritan theocracy in Massachusetts Bay and the Anglican establishment in Virginia.

In sum, it is fair to say that the framers of the Constitution designed a secular republic with religious liberty for all, but they did not want the government to be up for grabs by religions of any sort. Even before the adoption of the Establishment Clause of the First Amendment, Article VI declared that there shall be no religious test for holding national public office, a neutrality that had never before happened anywhere.

What, then, should be the functional role of religions in American public life? Religious leaders of all faiths have every right to speak their minds, as their consciences may dictate, on any public issue at any time. They even have the right to seek to make unlawful what their own faith deems sinful, though one may question their wisdom in so doing. But religious leaders enter the morass of politics at their peril. Clearly, they cannot be expected to be immune to challenge or criticism for whatever it is they advocate. This is particularly true if they seek to impose on others elements of their own doctrine that are not accepted by others. What is really needed is moral suasion and appeals to individual conscience, not the duress of secular law. (The abortion issue is a perfect case in point.)

Religions are repositories of traditional values; their leaders should be, first and foremost, practitioners as well as proponents of such values. Religious value teaching, both through example and through preachment, is badly needed in American public life, especially for our youth, the next generation of citizens. Many contemporary trends in our society are acutely unsettling to many people. The list is long and painful: the epidemic of violent crime, growth of the drug culture, emergence of a militant feminist movement, rising tide of divorce, soaring rate of teenage out-of-wedlock pregnancy, demand for abortion at will, breakdown of discipline in many public schools, growth of "gay liberation," and prevalence of X-rated movies, among others. There is a widespread conviction that things have gone too far, that liberty has become license, and that individual rights and freedoms have been exalted at the expense of equally important values, such as order, security, responsibility, civility, courtesy, and consideration for the rights, freedoms, and feelings of others.

Faced with serious social problems, many people yearn for the "good old days" (which often seem far better in memory than they were in reality), and want to believe that restoring organized public-school prayer and Bible reading and prohibiting abortion and pornography will somehow enable our society to cure its complex ills. They often seek scapegoats, blaming the Supreme Court, for example, for expelling God from the public schools. Hence the broad appeal of the so-called religious right and its simplistic rhetoric and remedies.

But moderate religious leaders, and others, who reject the ethos of the "religious right" have a serious responsibility to go beyond being naysayers. They need to advance positive, constructive alternatives. For instance, it would surely be useful to teach in public schools core values that are broadly shared by people of all faiths or none, on a non-sectarian basis—honesty, decency, sportsmanship, compassion, patriotism, respect and concern for the sensibilities of others. This kind of teaching can reinforce those parents and clergy who are striving to teach the very same values from a God-centered perspective, at home and in religious school, and also provide *some* moral guidance for those children who, regrettably, because they don't get it at home and don't attend any religious school, are not receiving *any* such guidance. Teaching consensus values effectively—but only *consensus* values—would do far more good than having children in public school parrot a prayer that has little meaning to most of them.

How should religions relate to government? In my view, all religions are most likely to flourish if they encourage government to keep its hands off, neither to hinder nor to help them. Any religion that cannot flourish without governmental assistance does not deserve to flourish. No religion should be beholden to government, but rather all should be free to bear prophetic witness against government, if events so require. Nor should government behave as if it were a church or a synagogue. It should not perform functions for its citizens that in their rightful free exercise of religion they are perfectly capable of performing for themselves without involving the machinery, property, or tax dollars of government. It is not a proper function of government, under our Constitution, to subsidize schools whose chief reason for being is to propagate a religious faith, whether the schools are Jewish, Catholic, Lutheran, Hare Krishna, or of any other faith. This is the predominant view among American Jews today.

My thinking on the role of religions in American public life has changed very little over the years, but there has been one change. When I was in law school in 1947, the U.S. Supreme Court decided *Everson* v. *Board of Education*, in which it upheld, under the First Amendment, public subsidy of bus transportation costs for parochial-school pupils. My view at the time was that this was a perfectly sound decision. Children are children, regardless of which school they may attend, and if government provides this benefit for public-school kids, why not for religious-school kids also?

What I did not see then and do see today is that public subsidy of transportation for religious pupils was not all that was at stake in *Everson*. Rather, that subsidy was an entering wedge for the pursuit of additional public subsidies for religious education. Next, for example, came the loan of secular textbooks to religious-school pupils, which the Supreme Court upheld in 1968 in *Board of Education* v. *Allen*. Each gain has been used as a precedent to rationalize further demands on the public till. "If A is constitutionally permissible, then why not B?" So the argument has been made, until what is sought today, in effect, is total public subsidy of religious-school education through a voucher system. I consider this a grave mistake on both constitutional and public-policy grounds, with potentially disastrous consequences for the principle of separation and for public education in America.

29

JOHN F. ROTHMANN

As a Jew in America, I believe that President Theodore Roosevelt was correct when he said, "Washington and his associates believed that it was essential to the existence of this Republic that there should never be any union of Church and State; and such union is partially accomplished wherever a given creed is aided by the State. . . . I hold that in this country there must be complete severance of Church and State; that public moneys shall not be used for the purpose of advancing any particular creed; and therefore that the public schools be non-sectarian." I remember well as a student in a public elementary school in San Francisco when Christmas carols such as "Silent Night" were taught to our class. I explained to my teacher why I would not sing the hymns of a faith that was not my own; fortunately, she understood. Later, as student-body president of my high school, I told the principal that I thought the traditional Christmas pageant was inappropriate for a public school. It was the last year the pageant was performed.

Still, I believe that religion has a significant role to play in American public life. While a majority of Jews in America, I among them, continue to be committed to the "wall of separation" between religion and state, it is important to remember that the separationist principle has never been absolute. Nor has been the American Jewish community's commitment to separationism. Jews in Amer-

John F. Rothmann, a Jewish communal leader in San Francisco, was a project consultant for *The Jews in America*, published in 1989 by Collins Publishers.

ica, as a community, fought for the right of rabbis to serve with priests and ministers as chaplains in the armed forces. Both houses of Congress, and our state legislatures, open with prayers offered by clergy of various faiths. Despite the commitment to separationism in other areas, American Jews have generally opposed legal efforts to challenge the constitutionality of tax exemptions for churches and synagogues. Moreover, although I am a "separationist" on some church-state issues, such as religion in the public schools, I personally do not oppose the temporary public display of a variety of religious symbols in the public square. In fact, I have been proud to support the efforts of the Lubavitch movement to place a menorah in San Francisco's Union Square during the Hanukkah season.

While I believe that religion and religious symbols play an important role within American public life, I recognize, and share, the concerns of those "strict separationists" within the American Jewish community who believe that religious freedom is most secure when church and state are wholly separated. An inviolable "wall of separation," it may be argued, is our best protection against amendments designed to write Christianity into the text of the Constitution, Sunday laws that disadvantage Jews, prayers in the public schools, and the like. In this 100th anniversary year of the 1892 Supreme Court decision *Church of the Holy Trinity* v. *United States*, wherein Justice David Brewer wrote that America was indeed a "Christian nation," it is appropriate to remember that as recently as the 1960s, Representative John B. Anderson of Illinois three times introduced in Congress a resolution proposing an amendment to the Constitution that read in part, "This Nation devoutly recognizes the authority and law of Jesus Christ, Savior and Ruler of nations, through whom we are bestowed the blessing of Almighty God." (Anderson, who was a third-party candidate for president in 1980, subsequently repudiated his efforts to write Jesus Christ into the Constitution.)

These examples are illustrative of the more than occasional efforts to misuse religion in public life, efforts that Jews in America should continue to guard against and oppose. While I am not an absolutist about church-state separation, I am concerned about the injection of any particular religion into our public life and institutions, and what this would mean for me as a Jew in America.

30

RICHARD L. RUBENSTEIN

IN 1964 I contributed an essay to a book entitled *Religion and the Public Order* (Donald Gianella, ed.) in which I strongly supported the absolute separation of church and state in the United States. Since then my views have changed.

The special need of a religious ministry for the military has long been recognized, and an equitable arrangement is in place to provide for it. However, other groups need some kind of religious ministry as well. Public-school pupils constitute such a group. Unfortunately, it is far more difficult to meet the religious needs of public-school students equitably. In the military, men and women are free to choose their denomination. Catholics, Baptists, Presbyterians, and Jews go their separate ways in matters of worship without creating a divisive problem for their normal work situation. Indeed, the fact that military service does not entail separation from one's own religious community probably strengthens individuals in their work.

Moreover, unlike children in their first years of schooling, men and women in the service can understand some of the ambiguities inherent in American religious pluralism. Separating children for the sake of prayer or worship could prove extremely divisive in public schools already divided by race and other factors. Further balkanizing of American public schools is hardly a good idea.

Richard L. Rubenstein is Robert O. Lawton Distinguished Professor of Religion at Florida State University. He serves as chairman of the Editorial Advisory Board of the *Washington Times*.

But it is also difficult to see how a common religious program might be worked out. If, for example, an agreement were reached that some sort of non-sectarian prayer be offered to begin classes or school assemblies, conservative Christians might take offense if Jesus were not mentioned. If Jesus *were* mentioned, Jews would feel excluded. Mutually acceptable references to God would in all likelihood be watered down to the point of irrelevance.

Nor is there likely to be agreement on Bible reading and the recitation of the Lord's Prayer in the public schools. The Lord's Prayer is among the most beautiful and meaningful ever uttered. However, in its original context in both Matthew and Luke, it is clearly a prayer that Jesus instructs his disciples to recite. As such, it is one of the most precious possessions of Christendom; but Jews are not disciples of Jesus, and it is impossible for them to recite the prayer while remaining faithful to their own tradition.

Similarly, the Bible has a different meaning for Jews and Christians. For Christians, the New Testament is not only part of Scripture, it is that part in terms of which the entire Bible is to be understood. For Jews, the New Testament is one of humanity's most important collections of religious writings, but it is simply not Scripture. If there is to be Bible reading in the schools, it is difficult to imagine that conservative Christians would accept the exclusion of the New Testament. If it is not excluded, Jews will be excluded.

Fundamentally, the problem comes down to the fact that Christianity makes supersessionary claims about Judaism that Jews cannot accept any more than Christians can accept the supersessionary claims Islam makes about Christianity. In the military this is not a serious problem, because the mutually exclusive religious claims are made within voluntary religious communities. In the public schools, even the reciting of the Lord's Prayer or the Bible involves taking sides for or against the supersessionary claims. What is private and non-divisive in the military becomes public and divisive in the public-school system.

Such considerations are of great importance to Jews because they want to participate as equals in American public life. Their historical experience has taught them that only when government is more or less neutral in religious matters is the ideal of civic equality likely to be achieved. Obviously, such equality will not be perfect. America was founded by Protestants, and culturally it remains very largely Protestant. Nevertheless, even the imperfect American approximation of equality has proven far more equitable than what is to be found elsewhere in the world.

Another difficulty in achieving a consensus on religion in public life is the fact that Will Herberg's tripartite description of American religious life no longer fits reality. When Herberg's book *Protestant, Catholic, Jew* was published in 1955, the mainline denominations, those most committed to interfaith dialogue and ecumenical consensus, were dominant within Protestantism. This is no longer the case. Millions of premillennial dispensationalists, fundamentalists, and pentecostals have achieved a measure of prestige and influence that Herberg could never have anticipated. These communities stress their exclusive religious claims and have little interest in ecumenical consensus. Moreover, the abortion controversy had yet to divide America. Similarly, American Judaism has changed radically since the fifties, with exclusivistic Orthodoxy far more influential today than ever before. In addition, there are now several million American Muslims and a growing number of American Buddhists. The religious needs of the latter communities cannot be met with Bible readings or nondenominational prayer.

Nevertheless, a completely secular school system is no longer a desirable option, if it ever was. When I wrote on church and state in 1964, there were far fewer single-parent families than today. In 1964, it was possible to suggest with some degree of confidence that religious training could best be left to the family. Unfortunately, the extraordinary rise in the number of single-parent families both above and below the poverty line has made it far less likely that the family can serve as the source of religious instruction for millions of young Americans.

If religion is completely absent from the training of millions of young Americans, that absence is bound to have a negative effect on their values. Religion is humanity's shield against anomie, that experience of absolute meaninglessness that dissolves all values, purpose, and hope. The absence of religion is already visible in the youth gangs, the drug culture, the family decay, the contempt for honest labor of too large a part of our population.

While religion is no panacea for the ills afflicting America, the absence of religion contributes to the worsening moral situation. Religious commitment has been one of the most powerful sources of behavioral discipline, literacy, learning, and a sense of vocation that humanity has ever known. The ideal of a "wall of separation" between church and state cannot be used to foster an ever greater secularization of American life. Even that ideal, which Roger Williams espoused long before Thomas Jefferson, was rooted in profound religious commitment.

Those with adequate resources are trying to solve the problem of religion and the school system by supporting their own schools. They should not be subject to the double taxation of supporting two school systems. Some formula for a tax rebate should be worked out for such parents in view of the fact that the burden on the public schools is lessened when their children attend private schools.

Nevertheless, the public schools will continue to educate a majority of America's young people. A way must be found to meet both the imperatives of a religiously pluralistic society and the religious needs of a growing number of Americans without any religious resources. Life is difficult enough for those in poverty without the further handicap of lack of contact with an institution capable of instilling values with which a person can achieve a heightened sense of discipline, dignity, and hope. (I am not suggesting, however, that only the poor are in need of greater religious involvement.) Certainly Jews must appreciate how crucial was the role played by the synagogue in giving the immigrant generation the values that permitted it to take an honorable place in the United States.

I have no concrete suggestions about how these contradictory imperatives can be met. Perhaps one place to begin would be in dialogue among religious leaders concerning the role of the public schools in overcoming the absence of values in a secular society. The needs are so urgent that one hopes at least the beginnings of a consensus can be reached. Without such a consensus, it is difficult to see how anything further can be done.

One thing is certain. Given the current crisis, the Jewish community cannot and should not bear the responsibility for excluding prayer or other expressions of religious life from the public schools.

31

JONATHAN D. SARNA

I N a petition to the Continental Congress, meeting in Philadelphia in 1787, the German-Jewish immigrant Jonas Phillips
enunciated what to my mind should still be the proper approach of
American Jews to the question of religion in American life. "The
Israeletes," he wrote, "will think them self happy to live under a
government where all Relegious societies are on an Eaquel footing."

Two centuries later, we know how difficult even this seemingly
simple goal has been to achieve. Equal footing, after all, clashes
with basic American notions of majority rule. Why should majority
faiths have to accommodate themselves to minority ones? Doesn't
democracy imply that it is the minority faiths that need to adapt?
While the First Amendment would seem to provide the answer to
these objections by limiting majority rule in the case of fundamental
freedoms, minority faiths in America know all too well that even
constitutional guarantees are not iron-clad.

Through the years, zealous legislators have, among other things,
forced Catholics to fund Protestant public schools, Jews to conform
to sectarian Sunday laws, non-Christians to recognize the national
holiday of Christmas, and Mormons and Indians to observe laws of
the state rather than the requirements of their faith. Had some
political leaders been successful, the Constitution itself would now

Jonathan D. Sarna is the Joseph H. and Belle R. Braun Professor of
American Jewish History at Brandeis University and the author of *American Jews and Church-State Relations: The Search for "Equal Footing."*

be Christian, complete with a Christological amendment that would, in effect, have made some Americans more equal than others.

It was on account of this zeal that many American Jews late in the nineteenth century abandoned their longstanding commitment to equal footing and forged a new alliance with advocates of strict church-state separation. Only a complete divorce between government and religion, they came to believe, could prevent the kind of abuses that would transform America into a bigoted Christian state. The "wall of separation between church and state" that Thomas Jefferson invoked in his famous 1802 letter to the Danbury Baptists became Jews' new rallying cry. In the twentieth century, led by lawyers like Leo Pfeffer, Jews and like-minded Americans fought through the courts to translate this ill-defined wall into a hardy bulwark of constitutional law.

Like many other American Jews, I grew up believing in this "Wall of Separation"—so much so that I was convinced it had been written into the Constitution itself. The justices of the Supreme Court in those days were our heroes. We cheered as they decided one case after another in "our favor," further separating religion from the state. Indeed, we fervently looked forward to the day when religion would be totally confined to home and house of worship, and the state would be divorced from religion altogether—better that, we believed, than state-sponsored Christianity.

What we did not know (how could we, it was not taught in our schools), and what I myself came to appreciate only much later, was how valuable and vital a force religion has been in American life. Anti-slavery, Progressive-era reforms, the civil-rights movement, the anti-Vietnam movement, the movement to aid Soviet Jews—all depended, in significant part, on religious activism within the public square. In addition, religious leaders have played a critical role (although, alas, not recently) in promoting high standards of ethics and morality. Historically, they have served as behavioral role models, speaking out fearlessly on behalf of "good government" and against social corruption. Were these, I asked myself, the kinds of activities that I wanted now to curtail by restricting religion to home and church?

More recently, it has struck me that the separationist ideal, essentially a theory of separate spheres, reflects an ideology that I and most of my friends have long since rejected. At one time, a large number of American Jews fervently believed that one should be a Jew at home and a person like everybody else on the outside. My generation, however, vigorously dissented from this view; we wore our Judaism on the outside too. Since we no longer confined our Judaism to home and house of worship (any more than we confined our wives to a "women's sphere"), had we any right to expect others to do differently? Clearly, the whole basis of "strict separation," with its assumption that religion and state should occupy completely different spheres of life, needed to be rethought.

Nevertheless, I today still worry about state-sponsored Christianity. I continue to fear that some of those who pay lip service to "religion in American life" really have in mind one religion—and not mine. I know that even today, more than two hundred years after the ratification of the First Amendment, many Americans would, given the chance, write their religion into American law.

But I also know that religions of every sort need to be nurtured in America. They strengthen the fabric of American life and promote social betterment. Strict separation is neither possible nor desirable. Religion is much too valuable and all-encompassing to be restricted to a "separate sphere" of its own. My own vision resembles instead the hope expressed by Jonas Phillips back in 1787: to live in an America where people of all faiths stand on an equal footing.

32

EDWARD S. SHAPIRO

G ROUP memory and individual experiences have convinced Jews that only an absolutist position regarding church and state furthers Jewish interests. Jews became citizens in Europe in the nineteenth century when the close ties between religious and political authority were severed. Many of the most treasured developments of modern Jewish history—the obliteration of the ghetto, emancipation, and social and economic mobility—resulted from the secularizing of politics.

Two aspects of the American Jewish political ethic have intensified the fears of Jews about religious involvement in the public realm. The first is a distrust of institutional authority and public officials, stemming from the Jewish experience with governments in Europe. Not surprisingly, a large percentage of the American Civil Liberties Union's lawyers and donors have been Jews. The second is a continual concern with the threat of anti-Semitism. Despite the sharp decline of anti-Semitism chronicled by public-opinion polls and by more impressionistic evidence, many Jews remain convinced that it has merely been driven underground and may surface in full force during the next economic or social crisis. This fear of American anti-Semitism is not limited to the Jewish man in the street. Even professors at Harvard Law School are not immune; see, for example, Alan Dershowitz's 1991 book *Chutzpah.*

Edward S. Shapiro is a professor of history at Seton Hall University, South Orange, N.J., and the author of *A Time for Healing: American Jewry Since World War II* (Johns Hopkins Press, 1992).

Such fears can sometimes cause Jews to see "anti-Semitism" where it simply does not exist. Many suspected that Jerry Falwell and his Moral Majority were anti-Semitic even though there was no evidence of this and, in fact, Falwell and his followers went out of their way to be friendly toward Jews and Israel. Christian groups that express concern over the plight of the Palestinians are automatically labeled anti-Semitic, though they might have good reason for thinking as they do.

The Jewish attitude toward church and state was shaped at a time when Jews were relatively powerless and outside the American cultural and political mainstream. Since the end of World War II, however, Jews have no longer been viewed as an exotic ethnic group, nor has Judaism been deemed one of America's many minor religious sects. As early as 1955, when Jews made up only 3 per cent of the U.S. population, Will Herberg in his book *Protestant, Catholic, Jew* noted that Americans considered Judaism one of the three legitimate expressions of the "American Way of Life." By then it was *de rigueur* for rabbis as well as priests and ministers to be invited to provide the appropriate blessings at public functions.

While Judaism was joining Protestantism and Catholicism in the pantheon of America's "great religions," individual Jews were ascending into some of the highest positions in American society, including the presidencies of Columbia and Princeton universities. In the 1980s, 8 per cent of the U.S. senators were Jews, as were, according to *Forbes* magazine, over 20 per cent of America's richest individuals. So prominent was the Jewish presence in American literature that, beginning in the 1960s, Gore Vidal, Truman Capote, and other malcontents began mumbling about a Jewish intellectual mafia that supposedly prevented worthy Gentiles from making the best-seller lists or getting the best tables at Elaine's.

Jews, however, in a remarkable display of what psychologists call "cognitive dissonance," continue to be dominated by the mindset of the outsider, refusing to admit the extent to which they have become part of the American establishment. A vital element in the self-image of Jews is that of the underdog and the alien, ever fearful of persecution by the dominant Christian culture. This helps account for the fears of Jews about the involvement of religion in public affairs, and for their reluctance to ask whether, in light of contemporary realities, this stance serves Jewish interests.

A public arena free of religion is, of course, impossible, if by religion we mean that which gives structure and meaning to life and is the source of ultimate values. The strict separationists argue that they wish to limit the intrusion of religion into the public sector; in fact, they really seek the triumph of a rival religion called secular liberalism.

Jews succeeded in America in part because they esteemed "middle-class" values in this the most middle-class of nations. They were frugal, sober, willing to defer gratification, morally conventional, aware of the benefits of education, and future-oriented. Jews played by the rules, at least by the rules that dominated American middle-class culture prior to the 1960s, and they reaped the rewards.

Religion has been a major bulwark of this "bourgeois" culture. Religion preaches abstinence and warns against a devotion to instant gratification. Since the 1960s, however, religion and middle-class culture have been under siege by a cult of utilitarianism, moral permissiveness, and extreme individualism. The prevailing philosophy of "do your own thing" emphasizes the rights, not the responsibilities, of citizenship. Public schooling has reached the point where mere attendance virtually guarantees promotion to the next grade. The defenders of abortion stress a woman's right to do with her body whatever she chooses. Under affirmative action, jobs and admissions to college need not be earned: they are awarded as a racial or ethnic entitlement. According to the ruling of a New Jersey judge, a homeless person has the right to frequent a public library even though his odor offends the library's other patrons and employees.

The religiously sanctioned middle-class culture that served Jews and other Americans so well has been gravely wounded. Nowhere is this more evident than in the recent census figures that reveal the dramatic disintegration of the traditional family. I doubt whether the moral and cultural decline of the traditional middle-class way of life can be reversed unless religion assumes a more prominent role. This means providing government funds for parochial schools. And it means taking seriously those clergy who still believe the "shall nots" are important, even when—and perhaps particularly when—the issues fall within the public square.

33

Marc D. Stern

THE jumping-off point for this symposium is the contention that Jews increasingly favor "equal time" in law and government programs that encourage the role of religion in public life. But both the poll evidence and the evidence of organizational behavior belie such a shift. No Jewish organization supported the Equal Access Act, which wrote the equal-time principle into law and allowed religious students a platform from which to inject religion into the public high-school environment. None supported giving creationism equal time with evolution. None supported ending the special status religious individuals enjoyed under the Free Exercise Clause in favor of a new rule that treats religious and non-religious citizens equally.

There are good reasons for the Jewish community's refusal to adopt equality as the overriding principle for defining religion's public role. Shortly after the Supreme Court upheld the equal-access law, fundamentalist and evangelical groups announced campaigns to spread the gospel in the public schools. Describing the decision, one group dedicated to encouraging that effort has written, "God has opened up a huge mission field. Our missionaries to this field must be our high school students. They can reach their generation for Jesus." Equality that encourages such activity is no boon to Jews.

Marc D. Stern is co-director of the Commission on Law and Social Action for the American Jewish Congress. He specializes in church-state litigation.

Some Orthodox groups have indeed sought to ensure "equal treatment or encouragement of religion in public life." That is surely true of the Lubavitch's campaign to erect menorahs at government sites, or of its support for moments of silent prayer, or, in the broader Orthodox community, of support for aid to parochial schools. These efforts represent the voice of, at most, 10 per cent of American Jewry. And the fact is that even within Orthodoxy there are sharp and deep disagreements about the wisdom of these efforts, of which only Lubavitch's really represents a desire to increase government involvement with religion. The rest of the Orthodox community is motivated by the very different principle of equality, or sheer necessity, not any independent judgment about the desirability of increased public involvement with religion.

In short, if there is any wholesale shift of Jewish opinion on church-state issues from a separationist point of view to an equal-treatment or greater-involvement point of view, it is not yet visible. It would indeed be startling if Jews were seeking to inject religion into the public life of the nation when for American Jewry as a whole religion has less significance than ever.

This is not to say that equality is not a value for most Jews. There is a unanimity that synagogues cannot be denied benefits accorded churches. Almost certainly, had the Supreme Court given unqualified approval to the display of crèches, Jews would have demanded equal treatment for menorahs. That demand would have represented not the view that it was healthy for government to be involved with religion, or that the public square needs greater input from religion, but the bedrock view of Jews that they should not allow themselves to be treated as second-class citizens. Equality between religious and non-religious, however, is simply not the only, or even the most important, value for American Jews.

What ought to be the role of religion in American public life? That question could mean three different things. It could refer to the problem of church-state relations—prayer in the schools, religious holiday observances, and the like. The current rule has on the whole served the Jewish community well. Beyond such pragmatic considerations lies an ethical one: it is right that in a society as diverse as this, government should not inject itself into religious matters. And it is hard to see any great benefit to religion from the use of opening prayers, "In God We Trust," or other ceremonial notations of religious influence. Such events only trivialize religion, contributing a patina of piety, not its reality.

Alternatively the question posed might mean to ask whether the government should show special tolerance toward religious practices by exempting them, if at all practicable, from restrictions imposed by laws of general applicability. Here the situation has been unsatisfactory ever since the Supreme Court's "peyote" decision (*Employment Division* v. *Smith*, 1990), which held that the Free Exercise Clause did not mandate such accommodation. The organized Jewish community was for many years not sufficiently interested in the problems of the religiously observant. If Rabbi Arthur Hertzberg is correct in describing the Jewish community as increasingly divorced from any substantial religious impulse (a description I believe to be correct), this lack of interest is hardly surprising.

But what I suspect the question means is yet a third thing: whether religious leaders ought to inject their religious views into political debates over the secular issues confronting society. Jews of all stripes in fact do just that: Orthodox Jews in the name of Halakah, Reform Jews under the rubric of the prophetic tradition. Even secular umbrella groups such as the National Jewish Community Relations Advisory Council invoke the Jewish tradition as justification for involvement in public affairs. Aside from a few early hypocritical denunciations of the religious right (and occasional critiques of anti-abortion activists) the Jewish community as a whole has not challenged such activity, even when it disagrees with the substance of what is said.

It is not at all clear that this involvement under the rubric of religion has much of an effect on the real world. Despite the celebratory claims of Allen Hertzke in *Representing God in Washington: The Role of Religious Lobbies in the American Polity*, I do not believe that American religious groups have any great impact on issues other than legislation directly affecting the religious community. At most, religious advocacy gives moral legitimacy to policy urged on other (secular) grounds. On rare occasions that may be significant, but these cases are only a small percentage of the matters in which a religious voice is heard.

There is uncertainty within the Jewish community over how far religious leaders should go in advocating religious positions. May they use religious language? What are appropriate means of speech? What claim do ministers have on their adherents, whether legislators or government officials? Governor Cuomo, and before him President Kennedy, insisted that the answer was easy—that other than in their private lives, the clergy had no claim to control the action of public officials.

The answer has the advantage of simplicity and of avoiding religious warfare and quasi-theocracies. But it also means that public officials must be religiously schizophrenic. Still, it seems advisable under present conditions for religious leaders as a matter of prudence not to seek to hold office-holders to religious discipline.

The debate over the appropriate role of religion in the public square was the most interesting church-state controversy of the 1980s. That it led to no clear answers is not particularly troubling. There are conflicting policies and pressures, involving a balance among competing interests of religious freedom, pluralism, freedom of speech, and civility. It is instructive that while Richard John Neuhaus made a manful effort in his *The Naked Public Square*, he was never quite able to explain—even, if I understand him correctly, to his own satisfaction—what the implementation of his thesis calling for greater religious involvement in the public square would mean for religious minorities. For Jews, that is no minor objection to advocacy of greater political activity by religious groups. Probably the best that we as a society can do is muddle through, with due regard for the conflicting interests.

In a way, however, the issue is an unfortunate distraction from more pressing realities. There is no lack of a religious voice in American society. There is a real lack of religious influence. In part, this is because of the give and take of the legislative process, a give and take for which the absolute commands of religious ethics are ill matched.

But the problem goes beyond that. It is that religion's pronouncements do not produce deep resonance. The question for churches is how to persuade people that their pronouncements are weighty and deserve implementation. How can religion speak to a society whose organs of communication are secular (and in which religious affairs receive relatively little coverage), a society whose values are pragmatic and short-term, where the commitment to religion is increasingly superficial, where most of the roles that religion once filled—whether setting moral standards, providing social services, or providing community—are now filled by groups and institutions in which religion doesn't play a significant role. The immediate problem, then, for religion is to persuade internally before turning to the public square. It is ultimately by persuading their adherents that religious groups will have influence, not by getting on the evening news.

I am not calling for a retreat into purely personal piety or a mystical insistence on communing with the Divine to the exclusion of all else. Nor do I believe that the secular world is corrupt and beyond redemption. Rather, the question is where struggles for religious influence should be fought—whether the primary forum ought to be the public square. The public square is attractive and beguiling; it offers mass audiences, and the illusion of fame. What it does not offer for religious leaders is a substantial chance of success. That lies in creating communities of believers.

This prescription depends on the existence of religious institutions with the wherewithal to demonstrate viable alternatives to the prevailing secular morality, and the legal freedom to implement those lifestyles as much as possible. Both of these preconditions are now in substantial doubt. Here, then, is the future of church-state relations. And on this turns the future of religious influence on the public square.

34

LANCE J. SUSSMAN

A MONG the religious and secular groups that advocate the invisibility of religion in American public life, few have been as
vigorous over the years as those based in the Jewish community.
For American Jews, the Establishment Clause of the First Amendment, which guarantees freedom *from* religion, is at least as important as the Constitution's promise of freedom *of* religion. Jews,
always a small minority, have been relentlessly persecuted over the
centuries by both statist and theocratic regimes. In the United
States today, the vast majority of Jews view the non-establishment
of religion as the foundation of their personal civil rights and of
Judaism's claim to legal equality. For American Jews, a benevolent
neutrality toward religion—i.e., "one nation under God"—is acceptable and even welcome, so long as the state does not, at any
level of government, officially incorporate religion or a religion into
its sphere of operation.

To some extent, American Jewish concern for religious invisibility
in the public arena grows out of Jewish theology as well as Jewish
history. The Jewish God is an invisible God. The second command-
ment, "You shall not make for yourself a sculptured image, or any
likeness of what is in the heavens above, or on the earth below, or
in the waters under the earth," has greatly restricted the role of
symbolism in Jewish art. The incarnation in Judaism is not in the

Lance J. Sussman, a rabbi at Temple Concord in Binghamton, N.Y., is
assistant professor of American Jewish history at the State University of
New York at Binghamton.

135

form of a human body but in the form of words. Unlike the cross, words are as powerful when heard but not seen as when they are heard and seen. Torah is an operant religious system; it is an artifact only in its most limited sense.

Several Jewish religious organizations, most notably Chabad-Lubavitch, a pietistic Brooklyn-based sect with a zealous outreach program, are currently challenging the American Jewish consensus on public religious invisibility. The Hanukkah menorah, they argue, is not a religious symbol but a cultural artifact. Thus they claim, rather disingenuously, that they are not raising church-state issues at all, that their claims are based on "freedom of speech" and not "freedom of religion."

Although the menorah campaign is making some headway in the courts, the majority of American Jews continue to oppose Lubavitch's efforts to raise Jewish consciousness by placing menorot in public places, and to consider such efforts both profane and dangerous to Jewish interests in this country. Public menorot will not only breed private Christian resentment, many American Jews are saying, but will undoubtedly open the door to the establishment of the faith of the majority, Christianity, as the official religion of the United States. For most American Jews, a national Christmas tree is wrong but tolerable, while the prospect of a compensatory national menorah is absolutely frightening. The majority of American Jews are convinced that public menorot will lead either to an anti-Semitic popular backlash or to a legal precedent for establishing Christianity as the religion of the land, or even to both.

While court cases over public menorot grab headlines, the deeper church-state concerns of American Jews involve the place of religion in public schools. For about a century now, no other issue in American Jewish life has evoked as much emotion and energy at the local level as the struggle to keep religion out of the schools. On school boards, at PTA meetings, and in private conversations with teachers and administrators, American Jews seem to be saying, "We will not let you do anything to the school environment that will redefine us without a fight."

Some compromises, however, are acceptable to American Jewish parents today. Winter instead of Christmas programs, which have the flavor of the season but little or no religious content, are thought permissible. "Our kids can participate," the logic goes, "and their kids won't notice the difference." They may also agree to the inclusion of Hanukkah cookies at a class party and even a Hanukkah song at the school's chorus program—usually a previously unknown and quite forgettable composition that emphasizes the ancient Maccabees' struggle for freedom of religion. Cookies and songs, however, are the limits of compensatory Jewish religious visibility in public space today for the vast majority of American Jews.

Despite the activities of Chabad and allied Jewish organizations, I detect in the mainstream of American Jewish society no movement away from a focused and narrow reading of the First Amendment's guarantee of freedom from religion. Nor do I see any awareness among American Jews of the irony inherent in religiously identifiable groups' arguing against the place of religion in public life. Indeed, the majority of American Jews actually expect and sometimes demand that their rabbis give religious sanction to keeping America secular. Their argument is not that of Isaac Backus and other colonial Baptists who wanted to keep religion out of the public arena in order to keep true religion safe from the pernicious influence of government. Rather, they are interested in protecting the security of their ethnic group, and they continue to maintain, often with great vehemence, that eternal religious invisibility in our public places is the "price of liberty."

35

AARON WILDAVSKY

"THE trouble is not," Milton Himmelfarb tells us elsewhere in this volume, "that religion in general has too small a role in American . . . life. The trouble is that a particular religion has too great a role—paganism." My comments constitute a gloss on his. I shall come at the subject from the viewpoint of another contributor to this symposium, Dennis Prager, who properly emphasizes his conclusion about "activist secular Jews." They "*are* highly religious," he says. "The problem is that their religion is not Judaism. It is liberalism." Via egalitarian liberalism we shall, properly instructed, come to paganism.

The trouble is that the word "liberal" doesn't do it any more. They are Korahites, these liberals, and they believe in equality of condition, not equality of opportunity. Neither equality under the law, nor equal access for religions to the public sphere, but only equal power and equal resources, will satisfy them. And that, I think, is why they become pagans.

When, as a teenager in New York City, I went to the Community Church to hear John Haynes Holmes and Donald Harrington give splendid liberal sermons, I soon realized that this was the next-to-last stop before a Jew became an atheist. (When I last visited a Unitarian church, the best that could be said for those who huddled together uncertainly on that Sunday morning was that they wor-

---

Aaron Wildavsky is Class of 1940 Professor of Political Science and Public Policy and a member of the Survey Research Center at the University of California at Berkeley. He is the author of *The Rise of Radical Egalitarianism* and *The Beleaguered Presidency*.

shiped feminism, that is, that they wished to reduce power differences between men and women.) The *last* stop was the Ethical Culture Society, which was as close to what fundamentalist Christians call "secular humanism" as one can get. I shall explain.

No social differences, no moral differences. People who cannot abide structure generally believe that human beings are born good but are corrupted by evil institutions. Structure, to them, is the work of the devil because it imposes differences among human beings who are naturally equal. So did Korah say that *all* the Hebrew people had received God's word, the revelation, and not Moses alone, so they were all entitled to interpret it as they saw fit, even if, as Korah recommended, they chose to return to the house of bondage in Egypt. Thus our liberal egalitarians come to see distinctions as artificial impositions by persons who wrongly claim authority over their fellows. All distinctions, as any deconstructionist will tell you, are suspect; they are likely to be arbitrary, illegitimate efforts of a privileged author or highfalutin text to impose its will unreasonably upon others. Better to be in perpetual revolt, to undermine all authority, to deny all distinction; a text read right to left or left to right would be equally meaningless, the affirmation and negation being contained in the same sentence.

How then to distinguish between right and wrong if distinction, distinction itself, is the enemy, justifying, as egalitarians believe it does, human oppression based on unconscionable inequalities? The greatest distinction in Judaism is, of course, the distinction between God and man, between what is forbidden and what is allowed. By that route, egalitarianism erodes all moral differences except those between the good egalitarian inner group and the evil hierarchical outer forces. Jews are commanded to separate themselves from the other nations by their peculiar practices, which are designed to inculcate, through endless social practice, the principles that one must not mix God and man, like wool and linen, or plough with different beasts, or mix diverse seeds, or, for that matter, boil a kid in its mother's milk, thus failing to differentiate a mother's love from sheer destruction. Everywhere Jews are urged to differentiate, and everywhere egalitarian liberals decry that differentiation. They believe, wrongly I think, that if they do not call attention to themselves but rather lose themselves in the undifferentiated mass, they will be safe.

Judaism is an observant religion. Its *mitzvot* abound with distinctions—between men and women, parents and children, Jews and Gentiles, whom you can have sex with and when, how you must and must not treat people under numerous circumstances, on and on. By viewing all these distinctions as based solely on power, radical egalitarianism makes Judaism immoral.

The politicization of most aspects of life would obliterate the distinctions around which Judaism revolves and without which it would amount to no more than remonstrations to be good. Judaism is a religion of differences, while egalitarianism creates a culture of diminishing differences.

36

RUTH R. WISSE

NOT long ago, on the campus of my university, I was talking to one of our activists, a professor who devotes much of her time to defending the rights of various academic constituencies. It is here relevant to note that this professor is an American and a non-Jewish Jew—that is, someone identifiably Jewish who underscores her disaffiliation from both the religious and the national content of Jewishness.

I was deploring what seemed a marked increase in the use of the classroom as a pulpit. Students were complaining of the promotion of political causes during regular class hours, a practice that had been mercifully slow in overtaking McGill. She nodded agreement. She herself, having lately complained to the building director about the presence in the lobby of a "Christian exhibit," had asked him to remove the offensive material. I was dumbfounded by this turn in the conversation. "How can you object to an exhibit?" I asked. "What was offensive about the material?" "It was religious material," she said. "That was offensive to me!"

I am not an American, and I cannot properly address the constitutional issues of church and state, but this chance conversation may help to explain why my thinking on the role of religion in public life has, indeed, changed. I had once assumed that liberalism was the guarantor of rights, only to discover that an illiberal

Ruth R. Wisse is professor of Yiddish literature at McGill University in Montreal and the author of *If I Am Not for Myself: The Liberal Betrayal of the Jews* (The Free Press, 1992).

liberalism could become the denier of rights. My objection to the doctrinaire university classroom, an objection influenced by the great Old Liberal Sidney Hook, takes for granted the right of everyone to promote his views, as long as the promoter is not empowered to deny the same freedom to others. But the New Liberal (my fellow professor to the core) defines freedom as the right to promote her views, and oppression as the attempt of others to express theirs. She regards religion as her special enemy, since its claim to speak in the name of ultimate Truth is the most serious challenge to her identical claim for irreligion.

Thus my defense of religion in public life is first and foremost a defense of religion against the illiberal liberal who would deny it the right of free speech. If religion enjoys no privileged place in American life, it should certainly be accorded its competitive place, its right of influence as well as of worship.

I would go even further. The way I judge ideas is not through their highest claim but through their lowest perversion. It is for this reason that Judaism seems to me a superior religion. Focused inward on containing man's capacity for evil through a pattern of small habits, it runs the risk of atrophying into dry ritual rather than enriching civilized life to the fullest—but that is the worst it does. I leave it to others to make their comparisons.

By the same token, I have come to trust the religious faith in God more than the liberal faith in Reason. At its best, the belief in a higher-than-human power breeds humility, which is the spiritual guarantor of tolerance. And even at its worst, every God-centered religion is at least open to the appeal to its highest transcendent principles. Contrarily, the evidence of our century suggests that the totalitarian impulse is implicit rather than accidental in doctrinaire irreligion that adores its shrunken vision of humankind. The difference between my illiberal colleague and a Communist commissar is only one of degree.

I am convinced that the uniquely democratic American Constitution could not have been conceived save under the aegis of God. Nor do I believe that American democracy can flourish without a sense of the God who inspired the Founders. It may seem bizarre, both to those who are religiously gifted and to those who deny the existence of God, to suggest that faith in the God of our ancestors can be a substitute for faith of one's own; but if the closest one can come to God is through what was fashioned in his Spirit, it is still sufficiently humbling. The appeal to God in the pledge of allegiance and the oath of office, in benedictions on ceremonial occasions, and even on the coin of the realm, is an attenuated but still vital reminder of the source of the American idea of freedom. I very much doubt that American freedom can survive without it.

37

NICHOLAS WOLFSON

I do not share the assumption that more Jews are having "second thoughts" about the relationship between church and state. In my own experience in organized Jewish life, I have seen no major shift. The mainstream liberal Jewish organizations continue to maintain the old position.

They do so with good reason. It is in the self-interest of minority religions to uphold the separation principle embedded in the First Amendment. Breach the constitutional barrier, and dominant religious forces will flood the schools and public life with the majoritarian religious beliefs of the day. There will soon be no breathing space for minority voices.

The core purpose of the First Amendment, whether in free speech or in religious expression and the separation principle, is to protect the minority from the oppression of the majority, no matter how sincerely or passionately the majority makes its claims. Indeed, in affairs of religion, passionate sincerity is present more often than not. In a democratic society, that passion will always lead to excesses, unless checked by the anti-majoritarian principles of the First Amendment.

I believe that some Jewish conservatives, or neo-conservatives, have been influenced by the 1980s rhetoric of Christian conservatives calling for the return to traditional values. The argument that

Nicholas Wolfson is a professor of law at the University of Connecticut School of Law. His most recent book is *Corporate First Amendment Rights and the SEC*. He serves on the executive committee of the National Jewish Community Relations Advisory Council.

144

morality in private life can be restored only if religion is returned to the public square is based on a kind of Aristotelian notion that the state has the opportunity and responsibility to develop a cohesive moral order. This is in conflict with modern libertarian ideas that men and women should be free, as John Stuart Mill put it, to express themselves in action so long as they do not harm others.

I do not share the conservative faith in the wisdom of the state. Modern experience with the cruel excesses of state power has taught us the value of government restraint in areas of personal belief and action. Belief in the beneficent role of government, intermixed with religion, embodies a nostalgic longing for an imagined pre-modern golden age where religious leaders led the common populace in a private (and public) life of piety centered in the happy nuclear family. If ever there was such a world—and I doubt that there was—it could not be introduced into modern Western society without coercive government suppression of heretical (as the government sees them) movements.

There is a passionate diversity in religious belief. For example, Orthodox Jewry, the Catholic leadership, and other religious orthodoxies belittle the role of women in religious leadership. Reform and Orthodox Jews and other religious groups differ deeply over the legitimacy of homosexuality. Reform and Orthodox Jews cannot even agree as to who is a Jew. Religious groups differ over the moral legitimacy of the use of military force. What religion, then, do we bring into the schools and American public life? The answer, tragically, will be, the religious belief that the dominant majority endorses.

Another obvious example of the dangers of religion in public life is the abortion issue. Catholic prelates, driven by fundamental belief, have threatened to excommunicate Catholic politicians who do not toe the line in this great debate. Fortunately, their effort at creating conformity appears to have failed. But their campaign is an indication of the kinds of censorship that will ultimately be brought to bear on minorities if religion is introduced as an instrument of proper belief into the schools and public life.

Unfortunately, Jews have only to look at Israel for a lesson in the dangers that religion in public life will bring. In Israel, Jews are the dominant majority. Under a complex set of laws and customs, religious leaders have a powerful grip on religious life in the public square. Marriage, divorce, and family life are largely subject to the dominant religious voices, which in Israel happen to be those of the Orthodox.

As a result, although Israel is the only democracy in the region, the freedoms we are accustomed to in the United States as a consequence of the First Amendment are diminished. My sense is that American Jews, and many citizens of Israel, are having second thoughts about this problem, which they view as equal in significance to the Israel-Palestinian issue.

38

WALTER S. WURZBURGER

FOR a long time I felt that any breach in the wall of separation between church and state would be detrimental and that religion should be confined to the home and religious institutions. I accepted the dogma that banishing all religion from the public arena would be in the best interests of Judaism. Because it was only in the wake of secularization that Jews were granted the benefits of citizenship previously denied to them in the Christian state, I assumed that the less religion there was in public life, the better it was for the Jews.

But several factors led me to begin to question this doctrine. For one thing, I came to realize that as a believing Jew I could not subscribe to the privatization of religious faith. The formula of the Haskalah movement—be a Jew only at home, and divest oneself of all Jewishness in public—could not be reconciled with Judaism, a religion that seeks to improve the world and establish the Kingdom of God, with justice and compassion for all.

To be sure, involvement in public life exposes religion to the danger of politicization. Every effort must be made to guard against this peril. But religion must not shirk its duty of providing moral guidance on matters of public policy that affect human welfare. Unquestionably, causes such as civil rights, the environment, and nuclear disarmament have enormously benefited from the involve-

Walter S. Wurzburger is rabbi of Congregation Shaaray Tefila in Lawrence, N.Y., and teaches philosophy at Yeshiva University. He served as the editor of *Tradition* for twenty-five years and is a past president of the Rabbinical Council of America and the Synagogue Council of America.

ment of religious leaders. If religion were to play a larger role in public life, we would not witness the indifference to the plight of the homeless and to other manifestations of want and misery that is so apparent in our current national ethos.

One may disagree with the position of the Catholic bishops on nuclear deterrence, or economic justice, or abortion, but they have every right to advocate their moral perceptions and indeed are duty-bound to do so. The fact that their moral positions were developed within the matrix of a religious value system should have no bearing upon their legitimacy. After all, the bishops make their case on the basis of moral rather than theological grounds. It hardly makes sense to take seriously the moral views of secular humanists while stigmatizing opposing views as theological and an intrusion of religion into the public arena.

In the days of the Enlightenment it made sense to contend that religious views should not be injected into the body politic, because it was taken for granted that all rational human beings were bound by an objective moral order. But conditions have changed drastically. There is no longer any moral consensus in an age that scoffs at moral objectivity and subscribes to moral relativism, if not outright nihilism. In the absence of a moral consensus, we have every right to advance our subjective moral perceptions, irrespective of whether they reflect a religious or a secular value system.

Utter secularization has been a disaster for the Jewish religion. Recent statistics indicate that large numbers of Jews have become totally alienated from their religious heritage. Our secular culture has exacted a tremendous toll in religious loyalties. It hardly makes sense for religiously committed Jews to be more apprehensive over the Christianization of America than over its complete domination by secular humanism. Rather than opposing state subsidies even for the secular studies at schools under religious sponsorship, we should welcome any assistance to our financially hard-pressed Jewish day schools.

In the light of current realities, the primary threat to religious liberty stems not so much from infringements of the Establishment Clause of the First Amendment as from disregard of the Free Exercise Clause, as in recent rulings of the Supreme Court. We are fighting the wrong war. We struggle against any weakening of the wall of separation between church and state—such as the display of religious symbols on public property or the granting of equal access to all religions in the public-school system—instead of fighting against court rulings that run roughshod over religious rights when they conflict with state interest. The attitude of the Supreme Court in *Goldman* v. *Weinberger* (denial of the right to wear a yarmulke) and in *Employment Division* v. *Smith* (failure to make exemption for the use of drugs in religious ceremonies) shows that the courts can no longer be relied upon to protect unpopular religious practices.

I, therefore, believe that many of the strategies employed by various Jewish organizations are obsolete. Instead of stretching to the limits the Establishment Clause and clamoring for an impenetrable wall of separation between church and state, we should concentrate upon protecting the Free Exercise Clause, thus insuring that unpopular religious practices, such as accommodating Sabbath observance and serving kosher food in public institutions, will be safeguarded.

While I oppose making an absolute out of the separation of church and state, I object to even nondenominational prayer in public schools. Any prayer that could satisfy the sensibilities of all children (including those who exercise their right to freedom *from* religion) would be devoid of genuine religious meaning, while at the same time it would infringe upon the religious freedom of some pupils.

What troubles me in the current trends in church-state relations is the vulnerability of religion in a society that is becoming increasingly hedonistic and materialistic. As the Rehnquist court demonstrates, there is a growing danger that the state may become increasingly entangled with religion, because "state interests" are permitted to override religious liberties. I am apprehensive lest the government interfere more and more with the free exercise of religion, especially as it intersects with public life, and find ways to curb the propagation of religious ideas that seem to run counter to the perceived national interest. I can imagine situations in which advocating aid to Israel would be interpreted as a kind of illegitimate political activity, punished by the loss of tax-exempt status for synagogues.

I urge the Jewish community to stop fretting over the presence of religious symbols in the public square and to direct its resources toward the protection of religious rights that are being eroded in a secular society in which religious tokenism is substituted for the genuine article.

Afterword
The Future of American Jewry

IRVING KRISTOL

FOR no other American ethnic group has the immigrant experience, including the experience of "Americanization," remained so vivid as for the Jews. Neither the Irish, the Italians, nor the Germans have produced a literature about this experience that is in any way comparable, in sheer bulk as well as in literary scope and scholarly depth. It is almost a century since the majority of Jews arrived on these shores, but the memories remain fresh—memories of economic hardship and economic success; of acculturation, assimilation, and the accompanying generational tensions; of triumphs and disappointments—sending your children to the nation's best universities and then watching them marry non-Jews.

Even in Israel, where immigration is so much more recent and the experience so much more traumatic, the past does not seem to be so present, so alive, so much in need of constant attention. The reason, of course, is that Jews in Israel feel that what immigration has done is to bring them "home." They do not doubt that they are where they ought to be, that the immigration experience is a narrative that comes to a proper—perhaps even a predestined—ending.

American Jews have no such sense of an ending. For them, the

Irving Kristol is publisher of *The National Interest*, co-editor of *The Public Interest*, and the author of, among other books, *Two Cheers for Capitalism* and *Reflections of a Neoconservative*. This essay first appeared in *Commentary*, August 1991, and is used by permission.

immigration experience continues, and it continues because they cannot decide whether or not America is "home." They think it is wonderful to be here, have no intention whatsoever of leaving for Israel or anywhere else, foresee their children and grandchildren and great-grandchildren as Americans—but somehow the idea of America as their "homeland" is one they find too slippery to cope with.

Not that they think they are in exile. An American Jew who goes to Israel, or who subscribes to the weekly edition of the *Jerusalem Post*, hears the status of American Jews described casually as "living in *galut*," "residing in the Diaspora." He hears those cant phrases but does not really listen to them. He has no sense whatsoever of living in *galut* or in something called the Diaspora—terms that American Jews under the age of twenty-five are not likely to comprehend. Indeed, it is probable that even among Israelis, those terms as applied to American Jews are by now empty of meaning, and are little more than linguistic survivals. Where, then, do American Jews live?

The answer, I would suggest, is that most American Jews see themselves as living in an imaginary country called "America." It was this imaginary country to which they migrated—in this respect they certainly differed from other immigrants—and their long "immigrant experience" is a narrative of how they coped with living in two countries at once: an ideal America and an all-too-real America. It is this extraordinary phenomenon that accounts for so many specific and unique features of American Jewry—the powerful inclination to liberal politics as well as the strident "alienation" visible, for a century now, of Jewish intellectuals, writers, and artists. There is a Yiddish expression that used to be in common usage, "America *goniff*," literally "America the thief," but in context meaning something like: "This is a wonderful country that takes as it gives." And so it does—as does life itself.

This dual life of American Jews was made possible by the fact that the ideal America and the actual America were in so many important respects convergent. The ideal America was (and is) indeed a homeland for American Jews, and the real America was sufficiently responsive to this ideal to encourage Jews to think of themselves as living in a homeland that existed *in potentia* if not yet in fact. The discrepancy between ideal and real, however, was always there, and existed to a degree that provoked Jews to a nervous and somewhat uneasy affirmation, as distinct from any easygoing and unequivocal one such as is to be found among other immigrant groups.

Most American Jews today are convinced—one should perhaps say they have persuaded themselves—that the trend toward convergence is stronger than ever. That is why they show signs of near-hysteria at any sign that suggests the contrary. The American Jewish community today is comfortable, secure, but lacking in self-confidence. It shows frequent symptoms of hypochondria and neurasthenia. It is a community very vulnerable to its own repressed anxieties and self-doubts.

An Exceptional Experience

It is right to be anxious because there are clear portents that we may, in fact, be entering an age of *divergence*, one in which the ideal America of the Jews will become more distant from the real America. But to get an insight into the processes of convergence and divergence, one must have a clear understanding of the fundamental forces at work. That understanding, it seems to me, is lacking because analysts of American Jewry look at their subject with a European paradigm in mind. But the United States is an exceptional country, and Jewish history elsewhere throws very little light on the American Jewish experience in the twentieth century.

What is it, precisely, that has defined this experience? Can one call it "assimilation"? The word itself seems so inappropriate that, while used freely to apply to German or French or British Jews, it is not used nearly so often to refer to their American counterparts. "Assimilation" suggests a strong, longstanding national culture, with a marked Christian complexion, into which Jews melt as they shed their distinctly Jewish characteristics. One of these characteristics, of course, is religion. That is why "assimilation" is generally associated with conversion to Christianity, either formal or informal (i.e., "passing" for a Christian without benefit of conversion). We have seen something like this happening in a relatively small percentage of the American Jewish population, but the overwhelming majority do not fit this mold. For "Americanization" is not at all the same thing as "assimilation." Nor is it the same thing as "acculturation." If American Jews, in the course of the twentieth century, have been "acculturated," so have all other Americans. American Jews have not changed more during this period than have American Catholics and American Protestants, of whatever ethnic groups. Moreover, they have all moved, gradually but ineluctably, in the same direction.

What is this direction? Toward a far greater religious toleration, obviously, which has cheered all Jewish hearts. But what, more exactly, has been the basis for this extraordinary (by all historical standards) flowering of religious toleration? Here two explanations are commonly offered, one seemingly anachronistic, the other lacking in self-understanding.

The first explanation has to do with the historical origins of religious toleration in the United States. It is a matter of record that such toleration emerged out of the struggle of various Protestant sects for the freedom to express their religious views publicly and to have their constituents and their religious establishments free from official discrimination. This is what happened in the eighteenth century and the first half of the nineteenth. It is fair to say, along with Richard John Neuhaus, that religious tolerance in the United States originally derived from the tension among a multiplicity of religious allegiances.

But after the Civil War, and especially after 1900, a quite different climate of tolerance gradually developed. This had to do with a decline of religious intensity overall and with the growing popularity of the view that "religion is a private affair," by which is meant a purely personal affair. Toleration became a matter of relations among persons, not among religious denominations. Indeed, individuals and communities that seemed "excessively" interested in their religious beliefs and allowed these beliefs to shape their lives in uncommon ways were (and still are) regarded as somewhat "deviant," and sometimes even alien to "the American creed." This "American Creed," now frequently referred to as our "civic religion," is a superficial and syncretistic compound of Judeo-Christian moral traditions with as much religious specificity as possible washed out. It is what John Dewey, the quintessential American philosopher of our century, meant by his phrase "a common faith," an overriding, nondenominational faith to which all denominations are loyal and subservient. This common faith is what we have come to call "liberalism," its exemplary institution being the American Civil Liberties Union. To the extent that such a common faith has prevailed, religious tolerance is not an issue worthy of debate. It simply makes no sense not to be tolerant.

Historians call this phase of our intellectual history, now more than a century old, "secularization," and they point to analogous developments in other lands to sustain the thesis that secularization is an integral part of modernization. It is impossible to argue with this thesis, for which the evidence is overwhelming. But it is possible and legitimate to question the explanatory power of the concept of secularization. Something important happened, that is certain. Secularization is doubtless as good a shorthand term as any to *describe* what happened. It is not, however, a useful concept if one wishes to *explain* what happened. For what we call secularization is an idea that makes sense only from a point of view that regards traditional religions as survivals that can, at best, be adapted to a non-religious society.

Emergence of Secular Humanism

When we look at secularization without an ideological *parti pris*, we can fairly—and more accurately, I would suggest—describe it as the victory of a new, emergent religious impulse over the traditional biblical religions that formed the framework of Western civilization. There is no mystery as to the identity of this new religious impulse. It is named, fairly and accurately, secular humanism. The mere fact that it incorporates the word "secular" in its self-identification does not mean that it cannot be seriously viewed as a competitive religion—though its adherents resent and resist any such ascription. Such resentment and resistance are, of course, a natural consequence of seeing the human world through "secularist" spectacles. Because secular humanism has, from the very beginning, incorporated the modern scientific view of the universe, it has always felt itself—and today still feels itself—"liberated" from any kind of religious perspective. But secular humanism is more than science, because it proceeds to make all kinds of inferences about the human condition and human possibilities that are not, in any authentic sense, scientific. Those inferences are metaphysical, and in the end theological.

There really is such a thing as secular humanism. The fact that many fundamentalist Protestants attack it in a mindless way, making it a kind of shibboleth, does not mean that it is, as some have been blandly saying, a straw man. It is not a straw man. As any respectable text in European intellectual history relates, "humanism," in the form of "Christian humanism," was born in the Renaissance, as a major shift occurred from an other-worldly to a this-worldly focus, and as a revived interest in Greco-Roman thought shouldered aside the narrow Christian-Aristotelian rationalism endorsed in the Church. At the same time, the Protestant Reformation weakened the Church as a religious institution and therewith undermined religious, intellectual, and moral authority in general. Christian humanism, moreover, did not long survive the near-simultaneous emergence of modern scientific modes of thinking about natural phenomena. By 1600, secular humanism as a coherent outlook was well defined—Francis Bacon exemplifies it perfectly—though it was careful not to expose itself too candidly, lest it attract hostility from still-powerful religious establishments, Protestant as well as Catholic.

What, specifically, were (and are) the teachings of this new philosophical-spiritual impulse? They can be summed up in one phrase: "Man makes himself." That is to say, the universe is bereft of transcendental meaning, it has no inherent teleology, and humanity has it within its power to comprehend natural phenomena and to control and manipulate them so as to improve the human estate. Creativity, once a divine prerogative, becomes a distinctly human one. It is in this context that the modern idea of progress is born, and the modern reality of "progressive" societies takes shape. These are societies dominated, not by tradition, but by a spirit of what F. A. Hayek calls "constructivism"—the self-confident application of rationality to all human problems, individual and social alike.

What is "secular" about this movement is the fact that, though many people still go to church or synagogue for psychological reasons (consolation, hope, fear), very few educated people actually think that their immortal souls are at stake as a result of their beliefs or actions. Man's immortal soul has been a victim of progress, replaced by the temporal "self"—which he explores in such sciences as psychology, all of which proceed without benefit of what, in traditional terms, was regarded as a religious dimension.

It is secular humanism that is the orthodox metaphysical-theological basis of the two modern political philosophies, socialism and liberalism. The two are continuous across the secular-humanist spectrum, with socialism being an atheistic, messianic extreme while liberalism is an agnostic, melioristic version. (This continuity explains why modern liberalism cannot help viewing its disagreement with socialism—with the "Left"—as a kind of family quarrel.) It is not only modern politics that has been shaped. Christianity and Judaism have been infiltrated and profoundly influenced by the spirit of secular humanism. There are moments when, listening to the sermons of bishops, priests, and rabbis, one has the distinct impression that Christianity and Judaism today are, for the most part, different traditional vehicles for conveying, in varying accents, the same (or at least very similar) sentiments and world views. Of other-worldly views there is very little expression, except among the minority who are discredited (and dismissed) as "fundamentalist" or "ultra-Orthodox."

The impact of secular humanism was far more striking among European Jews than among Christians. It was the secular-humanist Left, after all, that agitated for (and won) Jewish emancipation and Jewish civic equality. Moreover, emancipation unleashed within the Jewish community latent messianic passions that pointed to a new era of fraternal "universalism" of belief for mankind. What is now called "prophetic Judaism" gradually edged out "rabbinic Judaism"—the distinction itself being a derivative of the secular-humanist impulse. By the time the mass of Jews, mostly Central and East European, came to the United States, they were already secular-humanist in their politics—i.e., somewhere left of center—if not in other respects. And, in time, as American Christianity and American culture also absorbed this secular-humanist impulse, Jews were encouraged to become more secular-humanist in other respects as well. They located themselves on the cutting edge of American acculturation to secular humanism as an integral part of their own Americanization.

A Longstanding Liberalism

That Jews should be liberal-to-left in American politics is not surprising: they have always been so, and were ready to be so from the moment they set foot on these shores. What scholars and analysts take to be more interesting is that they remain so, even as they have prospered and achieved socioeconomic levels that, according to the socioeconomic determinism of contemporary sociology, should have made them more conservative. Aside from the fact that such determinism is always intellectually flawed to begin with, this overlooks the far more interesting phenomenon that American Jews not only have refused to become more conservative but have actually become more liberal-left in their thinking about non-political issues—what we today call "social" issues.

Take the question of abortion. The American people are divided on this issue, with 20 per cent or so on the permissive "left," another 20 per cent on the restrictive "right," and the majority flopping about between these extremes. Jews, over the years, have moved disproportionately close to the permissive pole. Why? Why on earth should Hadassah or the National Council of Jewish Women be so passionately in favor of a woman's "freedom to choose"? There is absolutely nothing in the Jewish tradition that favors such a radical inclination. Nor is there anything in the experience of most American Jewish women that would explain it. (Out-of-wedlock births among American Jews are among the lowest in the nation, and married Jewish women are expert at birth control.) It is purely an ideological phenomenon, a reflection of the power of secular humanism within the Jewish community. After all, if "man makes himself," why should he (or she) not have the authority to unmake himself, if it is convenient to do so? Abortion (except in cases of endangerment to the life of the mother) was long forbidden to Jews for religious reasons. Today it is taken to be permitted to Jews (always excepting the Orthodox) for religious reasons—but not Jewish religious reasons. Jews in America may belong to Jewish institutions, send their children to Sunday schools for Jewish instruction, proudly identify themselves as Jews—but their religion, for the most part, is Jewish only in its externals. At the core it is secular humanist.

Secular humanism seems very congenial to American Jews because it has assured them of an unparalleled degree of comfort and security. It has done so because Christians in America have been moving in exactly the same direction, if more tardily. A secular-humanist America is "good for Jews" since it makes nonsense of anti-Semitism, and permits individual Jews a civic equality and equality of opportunity undreamed of by previous Jewish generations. It is natural, therefore, for American Jews not only to accept secular-humanist doctrines but to be enthusiastic exponents of them. That explains why American Jews are so vigilant about removing all the signs and symbols of traditional religions from "the public square," so insistent that religion be merely a "private affair," so determined that separation of church and state be interpreted to mean the separation of all institutions from any signs of a connection with traditional religions. The spread of secular humanism throughout American life has been "good for Jews," no question about it. So the more, the better.

Well, perhaps this is a time for questioning whether more is better, and even whether what has been "good for Jews" will continue to be so. After all, the greatest single threat to the Jewish community today is not anti-Semitism but intermarriage, at a 30-40 per cent rate. The Reform and Conservative rabbinates confront this problem with strong talk about the importance of Jewish survival. But it is absurd to think that young Jews, as individuals, are going to make their marital decisions on the basis of ancestral piety—a theme that modern rationalism cannot take seriously. Even if these young Jews approve of Jewish survival, as many do, they find it easy to assign this particular task to others. And, of course, an awful lot of Jews, young and not-so-young, are less interested in Jewish survival than in the universal sovereignty of secular humanism, under which sovereignty Jews and Christians can live in fraternal peace, even though some may persist in older religious rituals that have a therapeutic value as they cope with the stresses of secular modernity. One sees many such Jews in Reform and Conservative synagogues during the High Holidays.

It is becoming ever more clear that what we are witnessing is not the advent of a brave new world in which religious orientation, like sexual orientation, will be largely a matter of taste. We are seeing, rather, the end of a major phase of American Jewish history, and of the history of Western civilization itself. American Jews, living in their suburban cocoons, are likely to be the last to know what is happening to them.

We have, in recent years, observed two major events that represent turning points in the history of the twentieth century. The first is the death of socialism, both as an ideal and as a political program, a death that has been duly recorded in our consciousness. The second is the collapse of secular humanism—the religious basis of socialism—as an ideal, but not yet as an ideological program, a way of life. The emphasis is on "not yet," for as the ideal is withering away, the real will sooner or later follow suit.

Two Flaws in Secular Humanism

If one looks back at the intellectual history of this century, one sees the rationalist religion of secular humanism gradually losing its credibility even as it marches triumphantly through the institutions of our society—through the schools, the courts, the churches, the media. This loss of credibility flows from two fundamental flaws in secular humanism.

First, the philosophical rationalism of secular humanism can, at best, provide us with a statement of the necessary assumptions of a moral code; it cannot deliver any such code itself. Moral codes evolve from the moral experience of communities, and can claim authority over behavior only to the degree that individuals are reared to look respectfully, even reverently, on the moral traditions of their forefathers. It is the function of religion to instill such respect and reverence. Morality does not belong to a scientific mode of thought, or to a philosophical mode, or even to a theological mode, but to a practical-juridical mode. One accepts a moral code on faith—not blind faith, but on the faith that one's ancestors, over the generations, were not fools, and that we have much to learn from them and their experience. Pure reason can offer a critique of moral beliefs, but it cannot engender them.

For a long time now, the Western world has been leading a kind of schizophrenic existence, with both a prevailing moral code inherited from the Judeo-Christian tradition and a set of secular-humanist beliefs about the nature and destiny of man to which that code is logically irrelevant. Inevitably, belief in the moral code has become more and more attenuated over time, as we have found ourselves baffled by the Nietzschean challenge: If God is really dead, by what authority do we say that any particular practice is prohibited or permitted? Pure reason alone cannot tell us that incest is wrong (so long as there are no offspring), and we have had the opportunity to see a network TV program called *Incest: The Last Taboo*. Pure reason cannot tell us that bestiality is wrong; indeed, the only argument against bestiality these days is that, since we cannot know whether animals enjoy it or not, it is a violation of "animal rights." Reform Judaism has even legitimated homosexuality as "an alternative lifestyle," and some Conservative Jews are trying desperately to figure out why they should not go along. The biblical prohibition, which is unequivocal, is no longer powerful enough to withstand the "why not?" of secular-humanist inquiry.

The consequence of such moral disarray is confusion about the single most important questions that adults face: "How shall we raise our children? What kind of moral example should we set? What moral instruction should we convey?" A society that is impotent before such questions will breed restless, turbulent generations that, confronting their own children, will see and find authoritative answers somewhere—somewhere, of some kind.

A second flaw in secular humanism is even more fundamental, since it is the source of a spiritual disarray that is at the root of moral chaos. If there is one indisputable fact about the human condition, it is that no community can survive if it is persuaded— or even if it suspects—that its members are leading meaningless lives in a meaningless universe. Ever since the beginnings of the Romantic movement, the history of Western thought for over a century and a half—in its philosophy, its poetry, its arts—has been a reaction to the implication of secular humanism that such meaninglessness is indeed the case. In fairness to secular humanism, we should say that it recognizes this challenge and encourages individuals to meet it through self-mastery and mastery over nature.

Human "autonomy" and human "creativity" are the prescription—
but this only makes the doctors feel smug while helping the patient
not at all. None of the powerful, interesting, and influential thinkers
of the twentieth century has remained loyal to secular humanism.
The three dominant philosophers of our age are Nietzsche, Heideg-
ger, and Sartre—a nihilist, a neopagan, an "anguished" existential-
ist. The main currents of thought in American universities today—
postmodernism, deconstruction, varieties of structuralism—are all
contemptuous of the universities' humanist heritage, which is dismissed as the accursed legacy of an "elite" of "dead white males."
Secular humanism is brain-dead even as its heart continues to pump
energy into all our institutions.

What does this portend for the future of American society? And
for the future of Jews in this society?

The situation of American Jews is complicated by the fact that
Israel, so crucial to the self-definition of American Jews, is facing
exactly the same kind of crisis in secular humanism. Israel, after all,
was founded by Jewish socialists for whom Judaism was but a
"cultural heritage." Most Israelis still regard themselves as secular—
but their secularism turns out to be different from, and more
vulnerable than, American Jewish secularism. The very fact that
their language is Hebrew and that their children read the Bible in
school makes a significant difference. Orthodoxy in Israel is not a
"saving remnant"; it is moving toward being the established religion of Israeli society, if not of the Israeli state, which remains
technically secular. One out of every twenty eighteen-year-olds in
Israel is studying in a yeshiva—i.e., is by American standards "ultra-
Orthodox." These give an indication of which way the winds are
blowing.

How will American Jews relate to this Israel? The answer, obviously, will depend on what happens to American society and to the
place of Jews in it.

A Return to Religion?

As the spirit of secular humanism loses its momentum, it is
reasonable to anticipate that religion will play a more central role
in American life. In theory, this religion need not be Christian. We

see today all sorts of neopagan impulses bubbling up from below, filling an aching spiritual void. On Mother's Day in 1991, a few dozen people gathered in Central Park and uttered prayers to "Mother Earth" and her associated goddesses. The *New York Times*, in an editorial, thought this a perfectly appropriate way to mark the occasion. In general, what is loosely called "New Age" thinking— our bookshops now have special sections for "New Age" litera- ture—represents versions of neopaganism, in which radical-feminist metaphysics plays an especially prominent role. Lesbianism, it turns out, is not so easily quarantined within the boundaries of an "alternative lifestyle."

Still, it is more reasonable to anticipate that the overwhelming majority of Americans, as they turn to religion, will turn to some version (perhaps in modified form) of Christianity. There is little point in speculating about the specific implications of any such development, but one general implication is unavoidable: as Amer- ican society becomes more Christian, less secular, the "wall of separation between church and state" will become more porous. In all probability, we shall see a turning back of the clock, with the place of religion in the American "public square" more like that which prevailed in the nineteenth century, as against the twentieth.

How will Jews react? In two ways, no doubt. The major Jewish organizations—including the majority of the rabbinate—will dig in their heels in defense of what we call a "liberal" society and "liberal" politics, by which is meant a society inclined to favor secular- humanist ideals and a corresponding set of official policies. At the same time, inevitably, Jews will perforce become "more Jewish"— which at the very least will mean a firmer integration into the Jewish community—as well as more observant, though not neces- sarily going all the way to strict Orthodoxy.

Is this picture of twenty-first-century America good or bad? Specifically, is it good for the Jews or bad for the Jews? The instinctive response of most Jews, committed to their secular liber- alism at least as fervently as to their Judaism, will be that it is not merely bad but desperately bleak. One does get the impression that many American Jews would rather see Judaism vanish through intermarriage than hear the president say something nice about Jesus Christ. But this instinctive response is likely to be irrelevant.

If America is going to become more Christian, Jews will have to adapt. That adaptation may involve changes in Jewish attitudes toward such matters as school prayer; it would also surely imply a greater sensitivity to Christian feelings than has been evident in certain Jewish organizations in recent years.

In historical perspective, none of this is of major importance. After all, in the decades prior to World War II, American Jews were a lot less militant in their insistence on a secularist society, were indeed quite prudent in their approach to issues that crossed Christian sensibilities. Such prudence can be relearned.

The key question, inevitably, is whether a less secular, more religious society will mean an increase in anti-Semitism. Not official anti-Semitism, of course, which has always been alien to American democracy, but the kind of economic and social discrimination that was common before World War II. It may be noted in passing that such discrimination did not prevent Jews from acquiring wealth, education, and influence. It created hurdles, but not impossible barriers. In any case, while there may be a revival of such discrimination, it is unlikely. In our increasingly multi-ethnic society, it is hard to see why hostility to Jews should be a ruling passion for large numbers of Americans, especially since Jews are now so firmly established in the mainstream of American life. Insofar as opinion polls can be trusted, Americans display little paranoid distrust of Jews, and in fact are less interested in them than most Jews imagine.

So it is reasonable to believe that Jews will continue to be nervously "at home" in America, though in ways congenial to the twenty-first century rather than the twentieth. The real danger is not from a revived Christianity, which American Jews (if they are sensible) can cope with, but from an upsurge of anti-biblical barbarism that will challenge Christianity, Judaism, and Western civilization altogether. The passing of secular humanism is already pointing to such a "shaking of the foundations." American Jews, alert to Christian anti-Semitism, are in danger of forgetting that it was the pagans—the Babylonians and the Romans—who destroyed the temples and twice imposed exile on the Jewish people.

Index of Names